waltz of the
asparagus people

the further adventures of piano girl

robin meloy goldsby

ISBN-13: 978-1456477547

ISBN-10: 1456477544

Library of Congress Control Number: 2010919207

This is a Bass Lion book, published in the United States.

www.basslionpublishing.com

Front cover image: © Doug Landreth/Science Faction/Corbis.

Author photograph by My-Linh Kunst, Berlin, Germany

www.kunst-photography.com

"Little Big Soul" lyric by Robin Meloy Goldsby and Jessica Gall, ©2010 Bass
Lion Publishing, BMI. All rights reserved. Used by permission.

Manufactured in the United States of America

Also by Robin Meloy Goldsby

❧

Books:

Piano Girl: A Memoir
Rhythm: A Novel

❧

Recordings:

Somewhere in Time
Twilight
Songs from the Castle
Hobo und die Waldfeen
Waltz of the Asparagus People

Table of Contents

To my friends on both sides of the Atlantic.
We may speak different languages,
but we hear the same music.

Author's Note

The stories in *Waltz of the Asparagus People* are true. I gave some of the characters and locations fictitious names and identifying features, and I reconstructed conversations to serve the dramatic flow. The music you might imagine while reading? That's 100 percent real.

PART ONE: VAMP UNTIL READY

Mr. President

Excuse me, I'm sorry. Excuse me. *Sorry, sorry, sorry.*

I maneuver across a crowded subway platform and step onto a slow-moving escalator. Perched in the middle, I avoid the sticky rubber handrails, and travel—head down, antennae up—until I emerge from the stuffy underground and step into the national-park spaciousness of Grand Central Station. I gaze at the terminal's star-spattered ceiling, shuffle around a clump of camera-toting tourists, and scoot outside into the June morning.

I live in Germany with my husband and children, but I spent my early adult years in New York City, playing the piano at the Grand Hyatt on Forty-second Street. I wrote a book, a memoir about performing in the no-star bars of five-star hotels—New York City lounges cloaked in jewel-toned velveteen—where I hid behind a Steinway in a shadowy corner playing *tinka, tinka, tinka*, hoping no one would yell at me for being too loud, too quirky, too disruptive, too musical. I was just another blond in a black dress, one of Manhattan's middle-tier musicians, good enough to make a decent living, but not quite good enough for anyone to notice.

America is indeed a great country—perhaps the only place in the world where a person can write a book about being ignored, and everyone pays attention. Today, as part of my accidental homecoming, I'm scheduled to appear on National Public Radio's *All Things Considered*.

Excuse me. I'm sorry. I keep bumping into people who know where they're going.

Pedestrians with bulging briefcases, backpacks, and assorted plastic shopping bags weave through a tapestry of street vendors selling African beads, battery-operated barking toys, and stale pretzels with spicy mustard.

NPR tapes the show in a studio on Second Avenue, not far from Grand Central. My flight from Frankfurt arrived late last night. Between the jet lag and my frazzled nerves, I'm in a dream-like state, something comparable to an early morning one-martini buzz. No olives.

I've forgotten it's impossible to walk in a straight line in this town. Once upon a time I had mastered the art of dodging, slithering, stepping-over, and occasionally tap-dancing through swarming city streets. But I'm out of practice; today's journey feels like a spooky ride in an amusement park. Plumes of smoke; brightly painted pop-up people who might as well be screaming *BOO*; sprays of water; splashes of God-knows-what; grime, guts, goo; and a man who yells, for no reason I can see, *bada, bada, bada*—all of these things confront me as I head to the corner of Lexington and Forty-second.

After a dozen years in the tranquil German countryside, waking every morning to a mind-numbing silence broken only by songbirds and church bells, I welcome today's audio jumble. I hear horns blaring, radios blasting Latino music, a jackhammer hammering into a thick slab of concrete, and a constant high-pitched squeal that sounds like microphone feedback.

Delivery trucks, taxicabs, gypsy cabs, fancy cars, jalopies, buses, and colorless vans with foggy windows clog the intersection. A silly-looking white limousine—the kind rumored to have a bathtub in the back seat—screeches to a halt inches from my feet. Anybody in there? Puff? Daddy?

"I'm tryin' to cross here!" screams an agitated pregnant woman pushing a baby stroller the size of a parade float. She balances on the curb and pounds on the side of the limo. "Don't block the box!"

The dark window slides down.

"Fuck you!" yells the driver—a woman in a tight black suit with a jaunty hat. She looks like an organ-grinder's monkey. "I'm runnin' a business here. Don't mess with me, lady. I got a gun. Keep your mitts off my car."

The light changes. *WALK WALK WALK* it blinks.

I wonder if *DON'T WALK* means you should run.

I cross the street. Most of the people heading toward me shout into cell phones and carry enormous bottles of water. They look too young, too thin, too thirsty. An old tissue blows up from the street and sticks to my right ankle. While avoiding a column of foul-smelling steam spewing from a manhole, I admire the high-heeled wobble of a woman in a pebbly pink Chanel suit. Where's she going?

Where is everybody going?

I check my watch, pick up my pace to avoid an old man throwing grain at a gathering of pigeons, and swat away the glittering confetti-like substance swirling around my head. It looks like stardust, but I'm sure it's not.

I wonder how I ever lived here, or why I ever left.

೦೦

The reason for the traffic jam becomes clear when I reach the corner of Second and Forty-second. Traffic has been diverted from the one-block area around the NPR building and funneled to the side streets. Must be someone important in the area. Or maybe there's a film crew on the block. As I look up, hoping to see Spider-Man dangling from a window ledge, I bump into Nina Lesowitz, the publicist for my book. I love Nina. She's optimistic, enthusiastic, and relentless. Everything a publicist should be. And ever so much more.

"Isn't it, like, exciting?" she says.

"What? The show? I'm pretty nervous."

"Forget the show! Someone important is here."

"Here? At NPR? Who?"

"Don't know who, security won't tell me. Maybe it's, like, Bush!"

"Oh, great."

"Maybe it's Mandela! Maybe it's Springsteen."

"I don't think they stop traffic for a musician, Nina."

"Maybe it's Streisand! Oh my God, I would die! Hey, what's on your jacket? You're sparkling. You're so funny!"

I'm reeling from fatigue, I'm getting a blister on my heel, and I need to forget about the mystery celebrity and focus on the task ahead. I'm concerned about being delightful on cue, especially in front of millions of listeners.

A beefy man with a clipboard checks off our names, looks at our identification, radios a message upstairs, and sends us into the lobby.

"Who's the celebrity?" Nina shouts over her shoulder. "I *hate* this. I just hate not knowing!"

"Can't say, ma'am. Sorry. Not allowed."

We take the elevator up to the studio. Hulking security guys in dark suits surround us.

"Oh. Oh. Oh. Who's it going to be?" Nina picks at the glitter on my jacket.

We're introduced to the sound engineer and told that my interview will be done as a remote, with Jennifer Ludden in Washington. I'm trying to stay cool, but the idea of a remote interview throws me off balance.

"Maybe it's, like, Cher!" says Nina.

I look over my list of talking points.

"Maybe it's, like, the Pope!"

The engineer adjusts my headset, and we do a quick level check on my voice.

"Maybe it's Paul and Heather!"

I notice a small coffee stain on my pants leg. At least this isn't television.

"Or, like, Dick!"

"Dick?" I ask.

"Cheney!"

"Oh. Yeah. Dick." My hands are sweating. And my throat is dry. "Nina, I could use a glass of water."

"Maybe it's, like, Madonna! Thank God I brought my camera. We gotta get photos!"

The engineer ushers Nina into the control room, and I do a meet-and-greet sound check with Jennifer in Washington. We're set to go. My face burns. I'm suffering from a severe case of imposter syndrome.

Just as the engineer prepares to start taping, Nina jumps up from her seat and waves her arms like a wild woman.

"Stand by, Robin," says the engineer through my headset.

Nina mouths words at me. Then she points into the lobby. I try to ignore her.

"Five, four, three, two——"

BILL CLINTON. That's what she's saying. I look through the thick glass wall and see his brilliant white hair behind a filing cabinet. It's either him or Santa.

"Rolling," says the engineer. Jennifer greets me. I respond in the media voice I've perfected over the past few months. Nina cranes her neck to see what's happening with Clinton. I feel like my brain has been split in half with an ax.

I cartwheel through the interview, managing to be mildly amusing in spite of the flop sweat dripping down my back. We pause for a minute while an assistant delivers an excerpt from the book for me to read. When the door opens I hear Clinton taping his interview in the studio next to me. He speaks eloquently about tsunami relief and the crisis in the Middle East.

We start rolling again, and I talk about playing the piano for a dental implant convention at the Marriott Marquis. *Tinka, tinka, tinka.*

I try, really I do, not to think about the former President of the United States sitting three feet away from me. During one of the breaks I'm tempted to knock on the wall, but I don't.

෴

After the show we're escorted to a lounge area and told not to touch the food. Nina immediately grabs a bagel.

"I'm starving," she says.

"Let's get out of here!" I say. We're expected at the Javits Center for a book signing and cocktail party.

"Are you crazy? We've got to wait. I absolutely must get my photo taken with Clinton." She pulls out her lipstick.

"Nina, they won't let us anywhere near him. And besides, I feel kind of funny about this. Maybe we should just go."

"Are you crazy? This is a once-in-a-lifetime opportunity. We're, like, staying."

We lurk outside the recording studio, having been given strict instructions to stay back once the President enters the room.

He enters.

Nina starts working her way to the front of the small crowd, tugging me along behind her.

The NPR staff gathers around the President, asking him witty and intelligent questions. Clinton responds while signing copies of his book. I've been around lots of celebrities in my life, but I've never seen anyone with so much charm. The fluorescent fixtures of the office cast a greenish glow over us, but he's a golden boy, dipped in a bucket of dawn-colored light. I glance over my shoulder, half expecting to see a special-effects technician hovering nearby.

Just then, he catches my eye, smiles, and nods.

"Can we get a photo, Mr. President?" says an NPR employee.

"Why, sure."

"Now's our chance," says Nina.

"Nina, we can't. This is for the NPR employees. We can't crash the photo op."

Next thing I know, I'm being shoved front and center and Nina is introducing us.

"Mr. President! This is Robin Goldsby!" says Nina. "She wrote a book! Just like you."

"How do you do, Mr. President?" I say. We shake hands. Now what? I panic, trying to think of something appropriate to say. Nice tie? Loved the bit about the tsunami? What?

9

Speaking too loudly and sounding very much like last year's third runner-up in the Miss Altoona beauty pageant, I come up with this: "Thank you, Mr. President, for everything you are doing to HELP OUR WORLD."

Silence.

"My pleasure," he says. "Where are you all from?"

"I'm from Cologne, Germany. But I'm American. This land is my land."

Silence. Where's Woody Guthrie when you need him?

"Cologne? Beautiful town. They have that big old cathedral there, don't they?"

"Yes," I say. "That's the Dom."

"The Dom?"

"The Dom."

Silence. I try to think of a fascinating tidbit of information to share with him. I lower my voice and lean in his direction. "You know, the Three Wise Men are buried there."

Silence. I have no idea if the Three Wise Men are buried there. Here's what I know about the Three Wise Men: Gold, frankincense, and myrrh. That's it. I know way more about the Three Tenors and the Three Stooges than I know about the Three Wise Men.

"How they got from Bethlehem to Cologne I can't imagine. Make a left at the manger and head north, I guess." I consider humming a chorus of "We Three Kings of Orient Are" but stop myself just in time.

"Wow, that's interesting. I never knew that," he says. "Hey Bernie, did you hear that? Those Three Wise Men are buried in that big old church in Cologne." Bernie writes something in a small notebook. President Clinton turns back to me. "So, you wrote a book?"

"Oh. Yes. It's called *Piano Girl*. About playing the piano in, you know, bars and lounges."

"And it's hysterical!" shouts Nina. *"She's* hysterical!"

"So you're a musician?" he says.

"Yes, Mr. President. Just like you," I say.

"And you're here pushing your book," he says.

"Yes, Mr. President. Just like you." I sound like a mynah bird. "By the way, I hear *your* book is really fabulous." I haven't heard this, but I figure it's a good thing to say.

"Thank you! Good luck to you."

"You, too, Mr. President."

I give him a copy of my book. Nina takes a photo of him with me. I take a photo of Nina with him. I sense she's about to invite him to go shoe shopping with us at Bloomingdale's, but his entourage whisks him into the elevator.

Right before the doors close, he waves at me. And then I hear him announce to his staff: "You know, those Three Wise Men are buried in that big old Cologne Cathedral."

There's silence in the NPR office.

"Really?" Nina asks me. "That's a riot!"

∽

We exit the building fifteen minutes later. President Clinton remains outside, shaking hands, posing for pictures, exchanging presidential pleasantries with surprised pedestrians. He flashes a smile at the adoring crowd and ducks into his limousine, one without a bathtub. Just before the door slams shut, I notice he's still carrying my book. His car zooms away with a police escort, and the traffic barricades come down. The bubble of quiet hanging over the block pops as cars begin rolling onto the empty avenue. As people return to their strollers, their cell phones, their water bottles, their pavement-pounding-purpose-pushing lives, the city's spirit rushes in like a raging river. *Bada, bada, bada.* It's almost a relief to hear the jackhammer.

Almost.

Hand-in-hand, Nina and I dash across the street and hail a cab.

"Where you goin'?" asks the driver.

"To the top!" shouts Nina. "But first we'll need to get to the Javits Center. Book Expo America."

"Don't know why, but traffic's a mess today," says the cabbie. "You gals would be better off taking the subway."

Naked

I've always been a big fan of the sauna. A good sauna can relax you, clear your head, and make your skin look great. And all of this for a mere fifteen minutes of sweating. Not a bad deal, when you think of it. I would love to go to a sauna right now, but I'm tangled in a web of German red tape and boxed in by stacks of moving cartons crowding our new apartment. I'm busy trying to unpack music books, learn how to pronounce *unbefristige-Aufenthaltserlaubnis* (the German version of a green card), and teach my son how to say *danke* to the cheese lady at the local market. A neighbor, sensing my need for a time out, tells me that the very pretty Sülztal Family Sauna is right up the hill from our home. I'm ready.

In Germany saunas are for naked people only. Bathing suits are *verboten*. Fine. But I'm an American woman. I'm fond of Lycra tank suits in dark colors, preferably with invisible lace-covered support panels. These days I worry that my six-pack looks more like a one-pack. A naked debut in public should be left to those on the prettier side of middle age.

Or?

One of the great things about moving to a foreign country is getting a chance to discover just how brainwashed we are by our own customs and traditions. The Germans pick wild mushrooms from the forest and eat raw pork for supper with no worry of falling into a trichinosis-induced coma. A lot of Americans—who would never ever touch a wild mushroom, let alone eat a piece of pig meat that hasn't been cooked in a blast furnace—eat peanut butter and bacon sandwiches and deep-fried Twinkies served on sticks. After just a few months in this country, I can see the German catalog of odd customs is just as wacky as its American counterpart. The trick, I suppose, is to figure out which American habits to toss and which German habits to adopt. Maybe the sauna would be a good place to start.

I've always worn a damp bathing suit in the sauna, because that's what we do in America. Never once, as I stepped into the tiny sauna at my New York City health club, did it occur to me that wearing a sticky garment in a sweatbox might not be a great idea. Maybe naked would be better. It would certainly be more comfortable. With this in mind I set off for the sauna. My husband stays home with our young son, who yells on my way out the door, "Get NAKEY, Mommy."

I enter the Sülztal Family Sauna—an oasis of tranquility tucked into a corner of meadow next to the *Autobahn*. I pay my fee for a day pass, tuck my hang-ups in the locker with my underpants, put on a bathrobe, and step through the heavy wooden door into an airy room filled with fountains, pools, and sunlight streaming through generous windows. There are men everywhere. Old men. Young men. Naked men. Water, water everywhere and not a gal in sight. I thought this was supposed to be a family place. The last time I saw this many naked men was at the Continental Baths, a gay men's health club in Manhattan that offered cabaret entertainment (Bette Midler! Peter Allen!) on the weekends. But most of those guys wore towels around their chiseled waistlines. The guys I'm looking at now, thick-bellied and heavy-balled, are not wearing towels. They stroll aimlessly, the way men do when visiting the home improvement center on a Saturday afternoon.

I try not to stare, really I do, but I've got a front-row seat at the Penis Parade, and it's a spectacle I've never seen before. These guys have other remarkable features, I'm sure, but all I see are penises. Fat ones, skinny ones, dangling and dazzling, the long and the short of it. Who knew there were so many varieties? And look! That penis marching toward the waterfall? It's wearing a little hat.

Flip, flop, flip, flop. The sound of the naked men's pool shoes flapping on the tile floor slaps me back to reality.

"Brauchen Sie Hilfe?" says a middle-aged man with a friendly penis. I mean smile. I have no idea what he's saying. In addition to my lack of German-language skills, I am also suffering from hysterical deafness.

I put on my very best face, the one I once wore when asking for assistance at the Chanel counter at Saks Fifth Avenue, cinch the belt on my bathrobe, look him in the penis, I mean eye, and say, "I am lost. Where is the door? You know. Door. Go outside." I am speaking in a very loud American Indian voice, the one I use when I think I'm talking to non-English speakers. I sound like Tonto.

"You are standing right next to it," he says, in perfect English. "Here, allow me." He is a gentleman with no pants on. He opens the door and I step through.

Olive trees and eucalyptus line the curved paths that wind through the landscaped garden. If it weren't for the naked men and the crisp November air, I'd feel as if I had entered a **Provençale** fantasyland. Or Oz.

Germans love fresh air, even when they're naked and the temperature is cold enough to stun a polar bear. I walk through the garden, shivering. I sneeze. This is ridiculous. I'm at a place that specializes in heat, and I'm out here freezing my ass off.

Hey, look at that guy there. The one with the blond penis, I mean hair. Well, that too. He looks like Sting.

I follow Sting because he looks like he knows where he's going. He jumps into a pool, and I continue on the circular path until I'm back at the entrance to the main building. I spot the steam room and peer through the glass door. Two women. No men. This I can handle.

I look over my shoulder to make sure no one is staring, remove my bathrobe, yank open the door, and enter the steam room. The two naked ladies acknowledge me with a hearty *"Guten Morgen."* In Germany, when you enter a bakery, the waiting room of the doctor's office, or a sauna full of buck-naked people, you are required by some mysterious code to shout out a greeting. Then you sit down and completely ignore everybody until it is time to leave, at which point you walk to the door and shout out a spirited goodbye. This custom can be particularly daunting for a foreigner. Especially a naked foreigner.

"Guten Morgen!" I yell back at them. Silence. I sit. I wait. The steam hisses and covers us in a translucent fog. The mist airbrushes my stomach wrinkles and the voices in my head are quiet. It's peaceful in here, a rain forest without the forest. Okay, maybe it's a tad too warm. Just a tad, but I'm coping.

The two other women stand and stretch. Before leaving, they turn on a hose and spray off the bench for the next guests. *What a nice country*, I think.

"Auf Wiedersehen," they shout.

"Auf Wiedersehen," I respond. I'm one of the crowd now. No one would ever guess I'm American. I'm just another naked *Frau* out for a steam.

It feels so luxurious, so decadent, being in this huge steam room all by myself. But warm. Very warm. Some might say hot. Boiling hot. Jesus Christ. Time to get out of here. I teeter toward the exit. Just as I reach the door, two barrel-chested men barge into the steam room.

"*Guten Morgen!*" they shout.

"*Guten Morgen!*" I say. Now what? If I remain standing I'm fully exposed.

I sit down. I cross my arms and my legs, hiding my private parts by turning myself into a human pretzel. I'm sweating like a *Schwein*. If I don't get out of here soon I'll faint. Shit, shit, shit. Worse than having these two guys see me naked in a steam bath would be to wake up in a German *Krankenwagon* with nothing on. Or what if I die from the heat and end up in the Nakey Morgue with a coroner making snide comments about my lack of muscle tone?

Enough.

Just as I'm about to flee, I remember that I'm obliged to spray off the goddamn bench. I grab the hose and turn on the faucet. The hose flies out of my hands and sprays one of the men in the face with cold water. He yells. The hose—which has a life of its own— writhes on the mosaic tiles like a snake in an Indiana Jones movie. I hit the floor and crawl around—buck-naked—wrestling with the hose as it jerks up and down.

So much for dignity.

Fuck fuck fuck fuck fuck sorry sorry sorry. I slide back toward the faucet. As I turn off the water I hear the men muttering something about foreigners. *There goes the neighborhood*, I imagine them saying.

I do not spray off my seat, and I do not shout a cheerful "*auf Wiedersehen*" as I drag myself out the door. I lean against the cool tiles of the shower area, gulping at the fresh air. For just a second, I forget that I'm naked. I notice my skin is as soft as a baby's behind. A middle-aged baby, but I'll take it.

೦೪

I learn to love my neighborhood sauna. I experience one minor setback when I turn on the automatic "back massager" in the outdoor cold-water swimming pool. It unleashes a powerful stream of water that catapults me like a nude Scud missile to the other side of the pool, right in front of the folks having lunch on the terrace. By the way, when the weather is warm, many of the diners are also naked. I haven't yet mustered up the courage for nakey dining. Somehow drinking a cup of hot coffee while topless doesn't seem like the wisest choice.

My husband now enjoys the sauna as much as I do. He has become an expert in the Sauna Step-over Technique, a tricky procedure that involves lifting one's leg and stepping over other naked people. Some folks recline in the sauna, and the step-over is the only way to get to the higher benches. Without the benefit of a bathing suit, or, at the very least, underpants, this can be difficult to master while maintaining a sense of decorum. Years will pass before I'm brave enough to attempt a step-over—I learn to look for a person with closed eyes, step lively, and try not to cough.

A decade after my first sauna experience I visit the brand-new Mediterana Sauna in Bergisch Gladbach, thirty minutes from my front door. Recently the Mediterana was voted one of the best spas in Europe. A day trip to this place seems like a mini-vacation. I'm particularly fond of the Himalaya Sauna, a golden-rose underground cave lined with 100 tons of healing salt crystal. The aromatic Candle Sauna offers a romantic view of the lake that borders the Mediterana property. The Rose Temple sauna smells like an English garden in mid-June. Heaven. It is the opposite of New York City.

During the regularly scheduled Mediterana *Aufguss* sessions, the sauna boy—muscular, shining with sweat, and wearing a plaid loincloth—comes into the sauna, drizzles a magic potion over the sauna rocks, and swings a towel over his head to circulate the aroma. There's a Greek God vibe to the routine, and some of these guys put on quite a show. Very quickly I learn to lean back so I don't get hit in the face with a wet towel.

Our kids, before they reach their adolescent years, will occasionally accompany us to the local sauna. Every so often I'll catch a glimpse of them wandering around naked with all the other naked people, and I'm stunned by their innocence and lack of modesty. They seem so European. Still, with two American parents, I don't imagine they'll be picking wild mushrooms or ordering the pork carpaccio at the local *Kneipe* any time soon.

I'm at home in the German sauna now, even though, deep down inside, I still feel slightly embarrassed—and very American—when I enter the land of the unclothed. I've stopped staring at penises, chasing hoses, and flinging myself across swimming pools. I don't know why the naked sauna was such a big deal for me in the first place. No one stares, no one cares, because naked, we all look pretty much the same—vulnerable, fragile, and flawed. Every so often I run into one of the gorgeous people, a Sting look-alike or a supermodel or a champion figure skater. We avoid eye contact and sit together and sweat. German or American, we all carry the weight of our nakedness, light as a feather, heavy as the past. Maybe it's a burden worth sharing.

"Get nakey, Mommy!"

Yes. Why not?

Waltz of the Asparagus People

New York City, 1986: One evening, on a break from my cocktail-piano job at the Grand Hyatt in Manhattan—a hotel that hosts Major League baseball teams, B-list celebrities, and an annual transvestite event called Night of a Thousand Queens—I notice an odd display in a glass showcase in the lobby. Inside the large window, built into a marble wall, is a handmade village of Asparagus People. Over 200 of them inhabit the village, each skinny green stalk hand-painted, shellacked, and dressed in a little outfit.

Good grief, I say to myself. *Are those things* real vegetables?

"Yep," says José, a muscular housekeeping guy who overhears me while sweeping the granite floor. "I helped paint the little fuckers. I never wanna see another asparagus as long as I live."

"Insane," I say to the bass player from the lobby trio. "Truly the work of a madman."

"Check it out," he replies. "That one has a briefcase."

"Back to work, pleeez," says Mr. Prang, the German Food and Beverage manager who patrols the lobby. "Do not stare at zee veg-e-tables."

"What's *his* problem?" I ask, as Mr. Prang spins on his heels and clip-clops away from us. His cleated shoes make a lot of noise on the sparkling granite floor. No one likes Mr. Prang very much. When he's not storming through the lobby, he stands behind a potted palm next to the crystal fountain and glares at anyone who crosses his path, almost like he's looking for someone to fire.

On the next break the saxophone player joins us at Asparagus Village. "Whoa. What a trip. It's like—uh—an international village. See that cat sitting on the motorcycle? He's wearing a sombrero. Dig the brother asparagus hangin' out the window—they painted his face black. And he's wearin' one of those little African hats. And that Asian asparagus chick on the lounge chair? She looks hot in that bikini. Yeow!"

Asparagus children play in the Asparagus Village sandbox, each with an expression of delight on its tiny face. In the back, asparagus policemen loom, wearing uniforms made of tiny scraps of brown fabric, with matching hats. The hats have badges.

"I told you," says Mr. Prang. "Do not stare at zee veg-e-tables."

I ignore Mr. Prang and spend every break peering into the village, thinking about the manual labor that must have gone into a display that's pretty much ignored by most of the tourists lumbering through the lobby.

"Look, Steve, an Asparagus Village."

"That's nice, hon." Night of a Thousand Queens might have captured the fancy of the overstuffed and bleary-eyed visitors parked in the Hyatt lounge, but Asparagus Village? Not so interesting. If you've come all the way to New York from Wisconsin, why spend your time checking out a hand-painted vegetable display when you can watch 1,000 guys dressed in prom gowns?

Every spring the village—with all-new costumes and themes—graces the Hyatt hallway. One year we enjoy Cowboys and Indians; the following season we're treated to an amusement park (including a Ferris wheel full of stoned-looking asparagus girls wearing shorts and halter tops); the next time around we marvel at an asparagus

Broadway show, complete with cast, pit orchestra, crew, and a chorus line of asparagus babes in skirts with red fringe. I fall in love with the whimsy and insanity of the display. But I never bother to ask why it's there.

Then, as is often the case in the hotel business, tragedy strikes. April arrives and Asparagus Village fails to appear in the showcase window. Several weeks later most of the hotel musicians are fired, causing me to wonder if all along there has been a strange correlation between asparagus and lounge music. I move on to the next gig and forget all about my skinny green friends.

∽

Bergisch Gladbach, Germany, 2009: Every April asparagus season begins in Germany, where I now work as a pianist at Schlosshotel Lerbach, a castle-hotel. The start of the season—trumpeted by the whoops of joy normally reserved for firework displays on the Rhine—marks the arrival of a two-month national frenzy. The Germans, anxious to tuck into that first bite of the stalky white "king of vegetables," hover in the produce aisles of local markets, discussing recipes for cream of asparagus soup. Until recently it has been hard to find homegrown green asparagus here; the Germans prefer the version rendered white by denying it sunlight.

I'm caught in the madness. As guests order platters of asparagus accompanied by baby potatoes, thinly sliced ham, and an obscene amount of hollandaise sauce, I check my watch and wonder how much notice the chef needs to time my dinner with my break. This is what happens when you leave New York City and move to the German countryside. You stop smoking and drinking and start

23

analyzing cooking times for vegetables. And if you're smart, you make friends with the chef.

Asparagus Village at the New York Hyatt flops back into my mind. Suddenly, it all makes sense. Here I am at the piano, playing "Spring Can Really Hang You Up the Most" for my hollandaise-guzzling guests, and I remember Mr. Prang, a guy I haven't thought of for decades. I can hear the cleats on his shiny black shoes, accompanied by the staccato rhythm of his accented English as he barked orders at all of us. He must have been the one who supervised the painting of the Asparagus People faces, coercing the baffled New York staff to draw miniscule eyebrow hairs onto asparagus stalks the size of a pinky finger. Maybe Mr. Prang helped with the task, muttering obscenities while painstakingly dressing each asparagus person. Maybe he was frustrated by the American lack of respect for his prized vegetable and dreamed of the day when he could escape to Europe in time for the start of asparagus season. Maybe he wasn't such a bad guy after all.

Maybe he was lonely.

I can see him now, beckoning his army of hopeful Asparagus People, persuading them to break out of their glass cage and march, run, and finally waltz through the hotel lobby, dodging the sharp ankles and clodhopper feet of dazed tourists and drag queens, rushing for the exit, lunging toward the fresh air, determined not to get caught and squashed in the revolving doors of a different culture.

The Fast Lane

Here I am, a blond American woman in a short skirt racing down a busy stretch of the German *Autobahn* at 150 kilometers an hour. I'm too busy driving to calculate the conversion, but I must be approaching 100 miles per hour. I negotiate a curve, my knuckles grip the steering wheel. I pick up speed and feel the G-force—or whatever it's called—push me back into my seat.

"*Überholen*," says the elderly man sitting in the passenger seat. "Pass the car in front of you."

"No, thank you," I say. "I'm going fast enough."

"*Überholen!*" he says.

"No! Please. *Bitte*." There are four of us in the sedan. I glance in the rearview mirror and see a smug-looking German official strapped into the seat next to my shocked and silent husband.

"You must do this," says the man next to me. "You will do it!"

With my heart racing faster than my speeding car, I overtake the silver Mercedes in the center lane.

"Now, was that so difficult?" he whispers. "I can see you are ready for the next challenge."

❧

This is not a scene from *The Bourne Identity*. This is the German Driver's Test—a complicated fifty-minute obstacle course that involves driving at high speeds on the *Autobahn*, parallel parking in a space the size of a paper towel, and manipulating a car through narrow European streets at rush hour while dodging grocery-laden pedestrians, bicyclists who insist on riding in the middle of the road, and small yipping dogs who should be on leashes but aren't.

Before moving to Germany, John and I were told that obtaining a driver's license here would be a simple matter of exchanging one license for another. It turns out that the rules—and there are a lot of rules—changed shortly before our arrival. Only citizens of European Union countries (and an odd smattering of American states like Wisconsin and Iowa) qualify for a license trade; those of us with New York State licenses must muddle through the system. This means numerous visits to modern offices with stern-looking administrators wearing designer eyeglasses in abstract shapes, an eight-hour *Unfall-sofortmaßnahme* (first aid) class, a tricky theoretical exam, and a fifty-minute hell ride with an official yelling commands in German, a language that, in spite of our twice-weekly lessons with Frau Ernst, continues to baffle us.

My dad taught me how to drive when I was sixteen years old. He owned a big old Chevy station wagon that cruised through Pittsburgh like it ruled the town. It almost drove itself.

"Here's the main thing," my dad used to say. "Speed. Think about speed. Whatever you do, *don't drive too fast*. And remember that every single car you encounter could have the likes of Mr. Phillips behind the wheel."

Mr. Phillips was the half-blind dry cleaner whose shop was on Mt. Washington, not far from our home. Dad warned us to dive into the bushes whenever we saw his car approaching. "Phillips!"

we would yell, leaping over shrubbery as he careened down Virginia Avenue, going way too fast and threatening to take out anyone not wearing a blaze orange vest and hat. Dad always said Phillips had a prescription windshield, but I think that was a joke.

Like every teenager in the city of Pittsburgh, I got my license by driving slowly around a parking lot with a chubby and very nice Pennsylvania State Trooper named Officer Mike, who offered me a rainbow-sprinkled donut after I completed the exam. The written test took only ten minutes and involved multiple-choice questions about what to do when you come to a stop sign and what the yellow light in the middle of a traffic signal means. Between my father's gentle instruction and Officer Mike's good nature, I snagged my license, ate my donut, and became—over the course of the next few years—a pretty good driver. I even learned how to make minor repairs to the car I was driving—impressing boys in the neighborhood with my ability to start my car's finicky engine by holding down something called the butterfly valve with a Popsicle stick.

My accidents were few and minor. When I was eighteen and driving a Plymouth Valiant I had a fender-bender with a Ford Pinto driven by an eighty-two-year-old man. Shaken, I went to his car and saw him slumped over the steering wheel. I honestly thought I had killed him, but he was just resting. When I was nineteen I drove under a bus when my brakes failed while driving down McCardle Roadway, a long hill that leads from Mt. Washington into the city of Pittsburgh. A policeman pulled me out of the car. My father came to rescue me, assuring me that crashing into the bus hadn't been my fault.

"There's a difference between driving too fast and driving without brakes," he said.

When I moved to New York City at the age of twenty-one, I traded my Pennsylvania license for a New York State license but gave up my car, choosing to take taxis rather than participate in the alternate-side-of-the-street-parking drill that took place every morning at the crack of dawn. Sleep-deprived, hungover, and pissed-off car owners would race from their apartment buildings at 7:55 a.m. Mondays, Wednesdays, and Fridays to move their vehicles—if they could remember where they parked them the night before—to the opposite side of the street. This highly volatile early morning bumper-car action cleared the curbs for street cleaners, who hardly ever showed up. So I became the taxi queen of Manhattan. In my peak years I spent upwards of $400 a month on cabs, a bargain compared to what some of my friends and neighbors were paying for the privilege of owning a car in the city.

With the exception of a couple of car rentals, I didn't drive for fifteen years. Instead I relied on my stable of cabdrivers, car services, boyfriends with cars, and—when I was dating a compulsive gambler with Atlantic City connections—the occasional Lincoln Town Car or stretch limousine with a driver in a uniform and a chilled bottle of good champagne at the ready.

I still wonder how I survived the taxicabs. Every night for over a decade I would step into the city's nocturnal traffic, raise my arm, and hope my taxi luck would hold for one more day. I had deaf drivers, drivers who claimed to speak three languages perfectly—but not English—and drivers who didn't know the location of Central Park. Some cabbies watched Spanish soap operas on little dashboard televisions while speeding up Madison Avenue; others flew down Fifth while counting their money and conducting heated radio discussions about Haitian politics. These rides always had soundtracks with booming bass lines—salsa or merengue, hip-hop or opera or bluegrass or jazz. Sometimes the music played in my head long after the ride was over.

"Hey! You're going too fast!" said my dad to a cabbie once. Dad had come to New York City to visit me and was hanging onto the plastic strap dangling from the ceiling of the taxi. "Slow down!"

"*Bada, bada, bada*," said the cabbie. He turned up the radio— was it Greek music?—and picked up speed.

On one bleary night in 1988, after a rehearsal for a musical that no one would ever see, I had a couple of vodka martinis with my friends. Sufficiently calm and happy, we stepped out of the bar onto the sidewalk along Eighth Avenue just as a cloudburst hit. A springtime Manhattan monsoon. We huddled on the sidewalk and cursed the sideways rain. The Broadway theaters had just let out, and there was taxi mayhem on Eighth. Trucks sprayed God knows what over the curb, and pedestrians dashed from one side of the street to the other with soggy newspapers covering their heads. It would have been a miracle to find a cab in that weather.

"What to do, what to do," said Andy.

"Another drink?" said Kenny.

"Allow me," I said. "I have good taxi karma." I stepped onto the avenue, raised my taxi arm with the right amount of flair, and out of nowhere, a Yellow Cab screeched to a halt. Kenny, Andy, and I decided to share the cab, since the likelihood of finding another one in the storm was slim. We slid inside, all three of us hunched in the back, our wet jeans sticking to the vinyl seat. I sat in the middle.

"Where you go?" said Jim the driver (possibly not his real name, but that's what his ID said). Back then I always liked to call drivers by their first names, I felt the *human connection* improved my chances of arriving at my destination in one piece. This was a lesson my mother taught me. Always make the *human connection*.

"Good evening, Jim," I said. "We'll be stopping first at Thirty-fourth and Twelfth and then heading over to the Upper East Side."

Jim sighed and pulled into traffic just as a large dark sedan sped past on the left and cut us off.

"Hey, you big motherfuck!" yelled Jim. He hit the accelerator, blasted his horn, and the chase was on. Andy and Kenny grabbed their plastic ceiling straps. I covered my eyes. Our car was going way too fast, threatening to hydroplane, and the three of us whipped back and forth and smashed against each other every time the cab swerved left or right. Finally, the brakes squealed and we came to a halt. The black sedan was next to us, wedged between the cab and a row of parked cars. The sedan's windows were tinted, and I couldn't see the driver.

"Big motherfuck," yelled Jim through the closed door of his cab. "Big, big motherfuck!'

Kenny and Andy slid to the floor of the cab.

"Get down," they yelled at me.

"Excuse me, Jim," I said. You really should just KEEP DRIVING. You never know. The man in that car might have a gun. New York City can be very dangerous."

Kenny stuck his head up from the floor. "Right!" he said. "Listen to her. She's right. That guy might have a gun."

"I got gun, too," said Jim. "I am professional killer in my country." And with that, Jim reached into the glove compartment and pulled out a pistol.

"Jesus Christ," yelled Kenny, pulling me back to the floor with him.

Jim got out of the car and slammed the door behind him.

"What do we do now?" I said.

"So much for your taxi karma," said Andy. "No wonder there was no one riding in this guy's cab. He's a trained assassin."

"What kind of trained assassin is named *Jim*, for God's sake?" said Kenny. "Is he a trained assassin from, like, Wales?"

"He doesn't sound Welsh," said Andy.

"Is he shooting?" I asked.

"I don't know, I don't hear any shots," said Kenny.

"That's because he's an *assassin*," said Andy. "He's probably using a silencer."

We couldn't see what was going on, but we heard a lot of shouting. Then Jim got back in the car, looked over the seat, and said, "What you do there on floor? No sex in my cab!"

"No, no, no sex!" I said, crawling back onto the seat. "Listen, Jim, we've decided we're hungry, so, uh, maybe we can just get out here, because—look—there's an all-night diner right across the street!"

"Oh yes," said Kenny, "they have the most divine meatloaf."

I meant to look at Jim's last name and ID number so we could file a report, but all I wanted to do was get away from him. I threw some bills on the front seat. We leaped out of the cab and ran across the street holding hands. We sat in the diner and thought about calling the police. Instead we had another drink and ate meatloaf. The rain eventually stopped. We found separate cabs and headed home.

Those days, thankfully, are over. Now I'm out of practice, I'm living in the land of expert drivers, and I need to get back in the driver's seat. From what I've heard the German Driver's Test is difficult. Officer Mike will probably not be waiting for me with a donut at the exam site.

I'm a little concerned about the stick-shift thing.

Like many American women, I've only driven cars with automatic transmissions. Okay, my mother can drive a stick shift and could probably drive an eighteen-wheeler, a train, or a stagecoach—just ask her—but she doesn't count, since she learned to drive before the automatic transmission became popular. Just about every man I've known has tried to convince me that driving an automatic isn't really driving—that the feel of the road can only be experienced with a stick shift. In most cases these are the same guys who enjoy spectator sports like boxing and American Gladiator, take vitamin pills with beer, and swear that with a little practice I'll be able to throw a baseball really far without dislocating my shoulder.

"Don't be such a girl," one of them—the compulsive gambler—told me. "It's *easy*. Here. You can practice on my car."

"Fine," I said, and took the wheel of his BMW convertible just outside of the Carnegie Deli. I drove a couple of blocks, then stalled out at the intersection of Fifty-seventh Street and Sixth Avenue, not only blocking the box, but creating one of those classic dumb-blond spectacles. Two screaming UPS men and a red-faced bus driver entered the fray, and, by the time I lurched my way out of the intersection, I had a bigger audience than most Off Broadway theaters on matinee day.

In Germany I've got little choice about the stick shift. Almost all cars here have standard transmissions. My American license—valid for a year after moving—is about to expire. I've been practicing basic driving skills on a used Citroën with a leaking roof and an automatic transmission. I *could* take the test with an automatic car, but then my license will forever limit me to an automatic—not such a good thing in Europe. John, who doesn't know about the

Manhattan BMW incident, convinces me that I am 100 percent capable of learning to drive a stick shift.

"It's easy," says John. "Just a matter of timing the clutch release."

"It's easy," says my mother on the telephone. "Don't be a wimp."

"It's easy," says my dad. "But whatever you do, don't drive too fast. And remember Phillips. There's someone like him in every country."

We buy a new car—a Volkswagen Passat station wagon—with a manual transmission. I prepare to join the ranks of stick-shift drivers.

Everyone applying for a license in Germany, regardless of age or previous driving experience, is required to attend an accredited *Fahrschule* (driver's school). These guys charge about thirty euros an hour for a lesson. A trainee isn't permitted to practice driving with anyone else but the *Fahrschule* instructor—none of this business of driving around the Walmart parking lot with your mother clutching the dashboard and slamming her foot into an imaginary brake. A student can practice only with the teacher, in the teacher's car.

Seems like a *Fahrschule* Mafia to me. Only the teacher can deem the student capable of taking the actual test, and the test itself must be taken in the *Fahrschule* car. A less-than-ethical instructor can clock a lot of extra hours by convincing vulnerable students they're not "ready." To get a license, an average student driver will typically spend upwards of 1,200 euros on training and test fees.

We don't want to get ripped off, so I ask my nineteen-year-old babysitter, who has recently passed the test, to recommend a teacher. She suggests a school in the neighborhood with a good reputation, run by an elderly man with Coke-bottle glasses, a froth of white hair, and a truckload of patience. He is a Phillips look-alike. We call him Magoo.

He's a nice guy, but I don't think Herr Magoo can actually see what he's doing. Maybe a semi-blind driving instructor isn't the greatest idea, but we sign up, mainly because Magoo seems fair, treats us with respect, and agrees to allow John—a skilled New York City stick-shift driver—to take the test with just one lesson. He thinks I might be ready after five or six hours of stick-shift training.

The cars used by *Fahrschule* teachers have double gas, brake, and clutch controls, allowing the instructor to override the trainee's bad judgment. The cars also have large signs that say FAHRSCHULE, turning the vehicle into a target for experienced drivers having a bad day.

I jerk-jerk-jerk my way around town while other drivers tailgate me, blink their lights, and honk their horns.

"Don't mind them, my dear. You're doing fine. Just keep the pace and stay calm." Magoo is the sweetest guy, even though he keeps calling me Frau Neu. "You take your time, Frau Neu," he says.

"Herr Magoo," I say. "I'm not Frau Neu. I'm Frau Goldsby."

"Yes," he says, "but you look like Frau Neu. Please forgive me."

Like a bat or a toddler's mother, Magoo seems to have built-in radar for dangerous situations. His dancing feet hover over his own clutch and brake pedals, taking action in dangerous situations. Gentleman that he is, he creates the illusion that I'm in control, and I start to think of myself as a pretty smooth driver, maybe even one of the boys, maybe even ready for baseball throwing and Manhattan intersections. Until we get to the hills. On our fourth lesson Magoo forces me away from the flat roads of the valley and up into the mountains, a novice stick-shift driver's worst nightmare.

Dozens of times the clutch slips, the car stalls and rolls backwards. Once I almost slide into a red Porsche while attempting to cross railroad tracks. While the words to "Teen Angel" run through my head, Magoo and his happy feet save the day. My Magoo is so brave; he never even gasps or utters an obscenity. Only once, in six lessons, does he lose his cool. We're exiting the *Autobahn*, and I stop where I should be yielding.

"My God, Frau Neu, you're going to kill us both."

I burst into tears. Magoo doesn't notice.

After my sixth lesson he proclaims me ready for the road test. First I must have my vision checked, attend the daylong *Unfall-Sofortmaßnahme* class—which includes resuscitating a rubber dummy named Manni—and pass the driver's theory test. Nervous about the German technical language, we pay extra for an English study guide and another fee to take the test in English. John fails the theory test the first time, because—in true guy fashion—he refuses to study the manual he has paid for. The manual, it turns out, is daunting, and the English, obviously translated by a non-native speaker, is counterintuitive. There are over 900 questions in the manual, many of them with photos and diagrams designed to baffle those of us suffering from hysterical comprehension disorder. But if I want the license I have to pass the test. So I hit the books and learn to answer questions like these:

- What is the maximum speed you are allowed to drive a truck with a permissible total mass of 3.0 tons on roads with one marked lane for each direction outside built-up areas? . . .

- How must a load be marked in darkness or bad visibility when it extends laterally more than 40 cm beyond the side-lights of the vehicle? . . .

- Your vehicle loses oil. How much drinking water can be polluted by a single drop of oil? . . .

༄

The day of the theory test, John goes with me so he can have a second try. This costs another 100 euros. I'm unsure of myself and sit next to him so I can copy, but the authorities give us separate tests. We both pass, which is a good thing since we're running out of money.

Now we're qualified to take the all-important road test. I'm dreading this. Magoo, having received the results of our written exams and permission to schedule back-to-back tests for husband and wife, arranges the date and time for our two-hour brush with divorce. Our slot is at eight on a Monday morning, not exactly a convenient time for a jazz musician and the mother of a two-year-old.

I'm still quite concerned about the stick shift. On the appointed day I wear a short skirt; if I strip the gears of the *Fahrschule* car, perhaps this will distract the officer in charge.

"Go ahead, wear the skirt," says John. He's a little miffed that I passed the theory test the first time and he didn't. "You need all the help you can get."

My stomach rumbles. John volunteers to go first. He sits in the front with Magoo; I sit in the back with Officer Schweinsteiger, our designated government driving official, a pleasant guy in a gray shirt who smells like the two packs of cigarettes he smoked the day before.

As John pulls into the morning traffic, Officer Schweinsteiger shouts orders in German, all of which John obeys. But halfway through the test—in between commands—Officer Schweinsteiger starts gossiping with Magoo. It becomes difficult—novices in German that we are—to distinguish the all-important Driver's Test command from the chitchat. Is he talking about FC Köln, last night's Westernhagen concert, or telling John to stop at the next corner? Hard to tell.

After fifty minutes of John's perfect driving, including fifteen minutes on the *Autobahn*, it's time to head back to home base. But something odd happens. With a twinkle in his eye, Officer Schweinsteiger begins yelling, "LEFT TURN! LEFT TURN! LEFT TURN!"

Don't fall for it, I think, because I can see the smirk on Schweinsteiger's face and, even though he may be an officer of the law, I know he's up to no good. I can also see the DO NO ENTER sign.

John turns left and drives the wrong way down a one-way street.

It's a trick, but there's nothing I can do. Also, there are cars headed in our direction, and I'm worried we're going to crash. I cover my eyes.

We do not crash. When we drive back into the parking lot, Officer Schweinsteiger grins and tells John he has failed the test. He tells him he needs more practice, that he doesn't swivel his head enough when merging on the *Autobahn*, and that he shouldn't drive the wrong way on one-way streets. John starts to defend himself, but really, it's difficult to argue that last point.

Now it's my turn. I think it's a silly waste of everyone's time. John is the best driver I know and he has failed. I am currently the worst driver I know, so what are my chances of passing? I'm upset for John and concerned for myself, and I just want to go home, play with my son, and drink a dozen cups of strong coffee. I feel stupid for being such a lousy driver. And I feel stupid for feeling so stupid.

There's a moment of petrol-scented silence as all four of us sit in the car, waiting for me to turn on the engine.

"Frau Neu?" says Magoo.

"It's Goldsby," I say.

"Sorry. Frau Goldsby, it's time for your test. Are you ready?"

"Yes," I say. "Let's do it."

Magoo pats my hand, signaling, in a Magoo kind of way, that everything will be okay. I pull out of the lot and the car stalls a handful of times. Onward. I drive two blocks with the emergency brake on and come close to a head-on collision with a garbage truck *on a hill*. All the while, I'm swiveling my head, looking out for Phillips, and making sure I don't go over the speed limit. Good.

Now it's time for the *Autobahn*. I merge and get us into the slow lane without an incident. I'm doing this. I am. I catch John's eye in the rearview mirror, hoping for a nod of compassion or pride or something. But he's busy trying to figure out how to stuff Schweinsteiger's head into the ashtray.

I cruise along in the slow lane until Magoo tells me to pass the car in front of me. I panic and say no. He uses his pedal to floor it. The speedometer reaches 140, and, because I have no choice, I clutch the steering wheel and pass the other drivers. I glance at John, who has snapped to attention. He doesn't know that Magoo has overridden my controls, and he thinks, as does Officer Schweinsteiger, that I've gotten into the fast lane all by myself.

Whatever you do, I hear my father saying, *don't drive too fast*.

But maybe this speed is just right. Officer Schweinsteiger grunts, which must be an encouraging sign.

John looks horrified, as if his nice slowpoke wife has been possessed by an evil *Autobahn* spirit and is now part of a miniskirted Formula 1 team.

Go, go, go. All on my own I keep up the speed and coast past the other cars in the slow lane. Magoo, Schweinsteiger, and John are my reluctant cheerleaders, coaxing me toward the exit with a conspiratorial silence.

It's easy, I say to myself. Before I know it, I've reached the *Ausfahrt*.

I pass the test. Whether this is due to my outfit, my expertise in head swiveling, or Officer Schweinsteiger's gratitude that I avoided a *Massenunfall*—massive pile-up—I have no idea. I don't say this out loud—divorce is not on this morning's agenda—but I like to think I've passed because I've managed to avoid driving the wrong way on a one-way street. Maybe I should suggest we go home and watch a boxing match or toss some baseballs around.

A week later John takes the road test again and passes. This costs another 200 euros and most likely saves our marriage. Guys don't like to be told they're lousy drivers. For that matter, neither do women, but we're used to it. By the way, if a student driver fails the test three times, he's required by law to seek the help of a German psychologist, one of the all-time great incentives for passing any kind of test.

I'm now the proud owner of a German Driver's License. It's candy-pink and the size of a passport and looks like a certificate of merit I once received in the seventh grade for swimming twenty-five laps of the Prospect Junior High School pool. Two years will pass before I'm comfortable driving a stick shift, during which time I'll remain convinced that the automatic transmission is one of world's finest inventions.

Sometimes, if you want to get where you have to go, you need to learn a few new tricks. Will I ever be one of the guys? Don't think so. Am I grateful to all the men who have contributed to my driver's education? Yes. Let's hear it for the boys. It took my dad, Phillips, Officer Mike, several hundred thrill rides piloted by an international squad of part-time taxi drivers—including a professional killer—a gambling man with a charming smile and a stalled BMW, a patient husband, Magoo, and Officer Schweinsteiger, but now I'm on my own, and I'm cruising.

Not too fast, not too slow. Just right. Next time I'm in Manhattan, I'm thinking about heading for Fifty-seventh and Sixth.

The Event Horizon

Time to put on my game face. I spend twenty minutes on makeup. Level-two eyes or level-three eyes? Better go with level three; otherwise my eyebrows will disappear and I'll look like a Martian. After I've blown every crinkle out of my longish hair, I put on my best formal dress—a Ralph Lauren ball gown with a skirt big enough to function as a circus tent. I purchased this 2,000-euro garment-for-a-queen at a Dutch factory outlet mall for €29.99, but no one needs to know that, at least not tonight. Jewelry or not? Not. It might get in the way. High heels or flats? Doesn't matter much because of the circus-tent dress, and since no one will be peeking under Ralph Lauren's taffeta creation, I go with the flats.

I've been summoned to an unfamiliar place—the Hans Arp Museum in Remagen—to play the piano for a rich man's birthday party. The midwinter night is clear and cold, and stars spatter the black slab of sky over the Agger River valley. The trip from here to Remagen should take about forty minutes. Kate, the *über*-polite English voice on my GPS, tells me how to get where I'm going. I marvel at the technology; the best minds in the world can't track down Osama bin Laden, but they're able to send a robot satellite into space that pinpoints my little Mazda and beams the information to Kate, who then tells me, in an obscenely civilized accent, which direction to turn.

I follow along, slightly nervous about the evening ahead, really nervous about getting lost along the way. Any musician will tell you: The job itself is the easy part; getting there is the challenge.

Turn left at the next intersection, Kate says. *Make a right, then take the freeway.*

I like that word, *freeway*. It sounds like a road where anything is possible.

Follow the freeway for 18.3 kilometers.

I can do that.

After eighteen kilometers, Kate says, *Prepare to exit right.*

No problem. Technology is amazing.

At the next light, turn right, then take the boat.

The boat?

Please take the boat, she says again.

Kate has obviously flipped out. I've read the stories of women driving into lakes and swamps just because the GPS told them to. I try to ignore Kate's directions. She argues for a few minutes, gives up, and fumes silently. After driving in circles and winding up in a dark alley, I decide to follow her instructions. So I head back to the turnoff, hum a few rounds of the *Gilligan's Island* theme song, coast down a ramp, and drive right onto a boat, which turns out to be a ferry.

I take a moment to gaze at the moonlit Rhine.

I'm a little confused. The Rhine is a very long river. There's no sign indicating the ferry's destination, and, even though I'm a big fondue fan, I'm afraid of ending up in Switzerland. So I rustle my skirts together and climb out of the car to ask the briny-looking skipper—who is, indeed, smoking a pipe—where we're headed. He looks at my big black ball gown, listens to my panicked German, points at the huge building on the opposite bank, and smiles. He'll take me where I need to go.

"But first," he says, "pull your car up to the front; we need room for the other cars."

"There are no other cars," I say.

"Could be a last-minute rush," he says.

I look at the flimsy rope serving as a barricade, the churning water just beyond—the Rhine has temporarily lost its romantic charm—and wonder if my gown might function as a lifeboat if necessary. I stuff myself and my skirt back into the car, turn on the motor, and move slowly forward, stopping a safe distance from the rope.

"A little more," says the Skipper.

I creep forward.

"More," he says, gesturing toward the river.

"That's close enough for me," I say.

He grins and puffs on his pipe.

Drive straight ahead and make a right, says Kate, who, along with the Skipper, seems determined to turn this evening into a *Poseidon Adventure* sequel, with me in the Shelley Winters role.

No other cars join us on the ferry. It's just Captain Bluebeard, Kate, my Mazda, and me, perched on the bow with the nose of the car inches away from the edge. I sink down in my seat and shiver. The things a girl will do for a job. For a moment I consider asking the Skipper if he will snap a picture of me on the bow of the boat as I do a Kate Winslet pose, but I feel scared to death for some reason.

Drive straight ahead, says Kate again.

"Oh, shut up," I say back to her. "How is it you know there's a boat, but you don't know there's a river?"

Drive straight ahead.

"No!" I look over at the Skipper. He's watching me talk to an empty car. I wave at him. He does not wave back.

The ferry takes five minutes to chug to the other side. I keep my eyes closed.

Drive straight ahead, says Kate after we've docked. *Then you have reached your destination.*

I park my car and head into the museum, a little frazzled but exactly on time. It's a beautiful place, full of bright colors and fussy people in dark clothes. I'm greeted by an event planner.

"Good evening, Mrs. Goldsby," she says in perfect English. "My name is Becky, and I'll be your assistant this evening."

Where was Becky twenty minutes ago when I was on the verge of plunging into the Rhine? Functions like this almost always provide an assistant for me. But outside of telling me where to hang my coat, the location of the piano, and how to get a cup of coffee on my break, I don't need a lot of help.

Becky looks like a Bond girl with a clipboard. I could fit four of her type under my skirt. She takes me to my dressing room. Since I've already got my ball gown on, there isn't much to do. We sit for a minute. I try to look like I'm meditating and preparing for my performance, but really I'm just wondering if my kids remembered to get the noodle casserole out of the oven. Becky is wearing one of those pop-star headset microphones, and she keeps pushing a button on her belt and muttering into it, apparently communicating with the captain of the event team. Or maybe with the Skipper.

"So. Are you ready?" Becky asks. She's way too perky and way too thin. I used to look like her.

"Yes."

"Goody!" she says. "I'll take you to the piano." We walk through the ballroom, weaving our way through miles of white linen. Tiny tea candles and huge orchid centerpieces adorn each table. The guests—there must be about two hundred of them—pay rapt attention to a chamber orchestra that's whizzing through a "Happy Birthday" arrangement, a classical extravaganza that results in loud cheering. I can't imagine hiring a chamber orchestra to play one song—least of all "Happy Birthday"—but I'm thrilled to see so many musicians working at one event. The twenty men, who are wearing tails, stand and take very formal bows. Wow, a six-minute gig. Cool. I'll be here for three hours. I wonder how much money they make for the six minutes. This is one of the quirks of the music business. Often you make more when you do less.

"Stand by," Becky says to me.

"Okay," I say. "Uh, where's the piano?"

"Behind the curtain, stage right," she says. "We can go back there now. Herr Teuscher will introduce you." As we head backstage the chamber orchestra files past us, led by three Bond-girl assistants. I still can't see the piano. I've requested a Steinway B, but who knows what I'll end up with. I hope it's in tune. I hope it has three legs. I hope it's a piano.

"This way, please, Mrs. Goldsby." Becky touches my arm and guides me behind the curtain.

"*Voilà*," she says. "I hope this is okay for you."

Thank God. It's the Steinway B. Some pianos are men; some are women. This one is a man. Solid, classy, forgiving. Just the kind of guy I like. My fingers are tingling.

I wait for Herr Teuscher—the guest of honor—to introduce me.

He invites me onstage. I stand next to him, a little embarrassed, while he says some nice things about my recordings. Then he tells everyone I'm here to provide high-quality background music and they should feel free to talk while I'm playing. They clap—for what, I don't know. I take a bow. I sit at the piano, put my hands on the keys, and everyone starts yapping. It's almost the reverse of a traditional concert. Okay, fine. This is how I make my living. As is my custom, I play for myself. On an instrument like this, it's a pleasure.

With tonight's starry sky in mind, I start with the Don McLean song "Vincent." Oh, this is nice. I forget the rest of the day, the drive to the gig, the boat, the volume of my skirt, Kate's annoying voice. I forget about Becky—her clipboard, her size-zero minidress, and her Madonna headset. I forget the audience, the orchids, and the reason I'm here. For a moment I even forget about the noodle casserole.

Then, as I continue to play, it all rushes back in, life-sounds organized into tidy whirlpools of melody. But there's something not quite right. The audience has stopped yapping. I glance over my shoulder to see what's going on. A curtain behind me has been pulled away to reveal a huge canvas, several stories high, with scaffolding in front of it. The canvas resembles a giant-scale version of the graph paper kids use for math problems. Each square is the size of a small windowpane. I don't know what's going on, and I wonder why Becky hasn't mentioned this to me. On her to-do list there must have been a note to warn me about scaffolding. I look for Becky in the wings, but she has disappeared.

A man wearing overalls and a black beret strolls onstage carrying a large bucket of paint. He climbs the scaffold. I don't know what else to do and there's no one around to ask, so I keep playing as he begins to work. With broad movements he covers the right quadrant of the canvas with slashes of bright red. The artist is a good five meters away from me, but I worry about paint splatters on the Steinway and my Ralph Lauren gown. I worry the artist will drop the bucket. Or that he might kick the bucket. I worry that I have found myself in the middle of a piece of performance art that could take all night.

The audience oohs and aahs but eventually forgets about the artist, the way they've forgotten about me. The artist's assistant—does everyone here have an assistant?—walks onstage, climbs the scaffolding, and hands him a bucket of purple paint. Wow. Yellow, then orange, then black. Then back to red again. Images blossom on the canvas, and, after multiple buckets of different colors, finer points begin to emerge. He's painting an outline of the museum, and look—there's the Rhine. He paints a dark blue sky, a full moon, and—with one quick flick of his wrist—scatters dozens of silvery stars across the acrylic horizon. He looks over at me, winks, and paints a few small music notes alongside the stars.

I play to accompany his painting. He paints to accompany my music. The audience eats and laughs and talks. At the end of two hours, when the painting is complete, the audience begins to applaud. The artist walks to the piano, extends his hand, and pulls me center stage.

"Hello," he says. "My name is Joachim."

"And I am Robin."

It's the first and last time we will talk to each other. We hold hands and bow. Herr Teuscher congratulates us. The guests eat tonka-bean ice cream on plates decorated with tiny swirls of dark chocolate.

Later in the evening the painting is dismantled into 200 individual squares. Joachim has presigned the back of each piece of canvas. Each person attending the party receives one part of the painting as a memento of the evening.

Herr Teuscher takes the stage again and says to his guests, "Each one of my friends adds something unique to my life, just as each stroke of color contributes to a painting and each note of music builds a song. Please take a part of this beautiful painting home with you, and remember that every single one of you contributes something meaningful to the canvas of my life."

Well.

I collect my coat—Becky has evidently ditched me for this evening—and head for the exit. Herr Teuscher, carrying one of the leftover squares, stops me before I reach the door.

"For you," he says, handing me the canvas, which is still slightly damp. "Thank you for your music. It was a lovely evening."

His assistant spots him talking to me and rushes to his side. "May I be of any assistance?" she asks him.

"Perhaps you could carry Mrs. Goldsby's painting to her car," he says.

"Thank you for the painting," I say to him. "And happy birthday!" But he's already walking away.

༄

The ferry ride back across the Rhine is quiet and dark; again, my car is the only one onboard. Clouds have covered the moon, the stars have slipped behind them, and giant snowflakes, the kind that look like children's paper cutouts, tumble over each other and land in geometric patterns on my windshield.

I step outside the car for a moment, hoping to feel the weight of the snowflakes on my face. I nod at the forlorn Skipper and look back at the lights shimmering inside the museum. With a soft thump the ferry bumps against the dock. I get back in the car, start the engine, and turn on the windshield wipers. In no time at all the snowflakes melt into each other and disappear. I drive down the ramp.

I wonder if what I've experienced has been beautiful or silly or a little of both. I turn on Kate, because I certainly don't want to get lost on a night like this.

Drive straight ahead, says Kate.

I'm headed home.

Marian McPartland:
The Lady Plays

Here's your coffee!" says Nina. "Rise and shine!" It's nine in the morning and Nina Lesowitz, my publisher's indefatigable publicist, has run to a Madison Avenue coffee shop to pick up breakfast for the two of us. I've come to town to tape a *Piano Girl* segment for *Marian McPartland's Piano Jazz* on NPR. The invitation to appear on Ms. McPartland's program came directly from the queen of jazz piano herself, and I'm honored, humbled, and very nervous. I flew from Germany to New York two days ago. Nina arrived yesterday from San Francisco. She has jet lag coming from one direction; I have it from the other. I figure between the two of us we have one complete brain.

During the long flight from Frankfurt to JFK, an elderly Indian woman wearing a bright pink sari sat next to me. Hardly more than fifty pounds, she had a face like a walnut and miniscule eyes with fluttering lashes. She sat in lotus position for eight hours without saying a word. Every so often she would hand me a little plastic container of coffee cream to open for her. She didn't smile or speak or acknowledge me in any other way—she would pass the cream to me and wait with one shriveled hand gently extended until I peeled off the aluminum top and passed it back. We went through this ritual at least six times. She poured her cream into numerous cups of tea, which she didn't drink. I suspected she was meditating, so I didn't interrupt her, because maybe, just maybe, she was keeping the plane in the sky. After we landed she stayed in her seat, legs crossed, palms resting on knees. I nodded farewell, stepped over her, and proceeded to the baggage claim, where I saw her once again, this time in a wheelchair pushed by an airline attendant. She was still in lotus position.

Today's taping will begin at noon. I have three hours to calm down and align my chakras, if I have them. I should have taken notes from my Indian friend.

My publisher is graciously funding this trip, but we're on a shoestring budget, so Nina and I are sharing a room. We're staying in the three-star Hotel Wolcott on Thirty-first Street. The hotel advertises itself as one of New York's "best kept hotel bargain secrets." The Wolcott's lobby—decorated in a pseudo-Baroque style with furniture donated by someone's Great Aunt Edna—teems with Eastern European tourists and American backpackers stuffing their bags with the free birthday-cake-sized muffins offered at the breakfast trough each morning. Nina and I have vowed to avoid the muffins and urban backpackers whenever possible.

Hotel Wolcott is a fine establishment, but the two of us, self-proclaimed travel princesses, are used to places with heated towels, L'Occitane de Provence toiletries, and working elevators. Low-budget or not, we're determined to have fun, so we cheerfully climb the four flights of steps several times each day, swearing we can feel ourselves slimming down. We hang the towels on the radiator and buy our own overpriced toiletries. The hotel must be trying to attract visiting NBA teams with the height of its bathroom mirrors. I put a little stool in the bathroom so we can boost ourselves up over the sink to put on makeup. Every night we examine the mattresses for signs of bedbugs, a growing problem in New York City hotels. We've decided Hotel Wolcott is unusually clean for one of these budget places. Still, I've been spraying tea-tree oil on the bed linens, just in case.

"Hey, look at this," says Nina. She's sipping coffee and browsing through the hotel brochure. "We can book our next press event downstairs at the Buddy Holly Conference Center. He stayed here in 1958. Go figure. Let's see, the room features, uh, a table and eight chairs. And lights. They have lights."

I'm still in bed, wondering if I should drink the coffee or not drink the coffee. I need it to wake up, but my nerves are shot and the caffeine certainly won't help.

Awake and nervous is better than calm and comatose. I drink the coffee.

"God, I hate this," I say.

"What?"

"I'm nervous. I hate feeling this way. You should have let me sleep until twenty minutes before the taping. Then I wouldn't have to spend the next three hours feeling sick."

"Yeah, but then you wouldn't have time to do your hair."

"Nina, it's radio. Hair doesn't matter."

"Hair *always* matters. We might want to take photos. I have to get a shot of you with Marian! Last time we were together we met, like, Bill Clinton. *Hello?* Who knows what will happen today? I've heard Beyoncé is in town. We want to look nice. And it will take a while to get ready in this place. The shower needs twenty minutes to warm up—I timed it yesterday. I turned the shower on, went out for coffee, and when I came back twenty minutes later it was finally warm. And I think the hairdryer is from 1959."

"Maybe it was Buddy Holly's hair dryer."

"Eat a bagel, you'll feel better."

It's true. New York City bagels always make me feel better.

"I don't think they had hair dryers in 1959."

"How do you think Buddy Holly got his hair to do that? It doesn't matter—you're going to be fine!" Nina says. "Once you're dressed we'll go shopping for accessories."

"Accessories?"

"Junk jewelry. We're in the junk-jewelry district—the world capital for junk jewelry. God, I *love* New York."

"Nina, I've got to concentrate on the show, I'm freaked out, and you want me to go shopping for jewelry an hour before the session?"

"It's a perfect solution," she says. "You can't shop and be nervous at the same time. Besides, you've been practicing for, what, thirty-five years? If you're not ready now, you'll never be ready."

"Right," I say. She has a point. I'm happy Nina is here. She distracts me; she makes me laugh. She's keeping the plane in the sky.

෨෨

I follow Nina into the nearest junk-jewelry store.

"They say you need a wholesale license to shop here, but just grab a basket and act like you know what you're doing," Nina says.

"I'm good at that," I say.

"Look! Emeralds! These earrings would be perfect with that black sweater you wore last night. They're so adorable."

I need fake emerald earrings like I need a dogsled, but I throw them in my basket and wander around the store. Garlands of fake diamonds and other dangling bits of glitz hang from the velvet-covered walls. The fluorescent lights bounce off the plastic gems and mirrors and send reflections back and forth across the shop. I feel as if I'm trapped inside a disco ball. I double-check my backpack to make sure I've remembered the music charts I've written out for Marian—we're scheduled to play three duets in addition to my four solo pieces. The show, which is recorded months in advance, will be edited to fit the one-hour NPR time slot.

"Look, Robin!" says Nina. "A tiara with feathers!"

I grab a rhinestone bracelet and a couple of rings for my daughter.

"What time is it, Nina? Time to go?"

"Nope. We still have thirty minutes. Look over there at those darling African beads. Very cool."

My cell phone rings. It's John calling from Germany to wish me luck. It's five-thirty in the morning there.

"You'll be fine," he says. "Remember to breathe. Where are you now?"

"I'm in a junk-jewelry store called Nick's Picks. Nina is trying to keep me distracted."

"Good. Listen to her. She knows what she's doing. Better that you're in a junk-jewelry store than, say, Bergdorf Goodman."

I've been a fan of Marian's show for years. *Piano Jazz* is the longest-running cultural program on National Public Radio. The NPR affiliate in Berlin airs it every week, so for the past decade I've been listening on Saturday evenings when I'm driving home from my piano job. Marian plays with guts but never relinquishes her femininity. She connects the gap between sensitivity and strength, playing with conviction and vulnerability, wit and intelligence, innocence and maturity. Her relaxed interview style is not unlike her playing. She has been in the USA for most of her adult life, yet she maintains an air of English graciousness—treating each guest like a long-lost best friend, using her warm and smoky voice to invite the listener into her living room for a little music and a cocktail or two.

"She has played with, like, everyone," says Nina as she scoops up a handful of fake ruby hair ornaments. "Oscar Peterson, George Shearing, Bill Evans, and well, the list goes on and on. She even had Clint Eastwood on the show. You know, he plays the piano."

Nina has done her publicist homework.

"Oh, Nina, stop. This is making me more nervous."

"Sorry."

"That's okay."

Silence.

"Alicia Keys and Tony Bennett and, what's his name? The blind guy—you know who I mean."

"Stevie?"

"No, the other one."

"Ray?"

"Oh yeah, Ray Charles. I love him! He was on the show, too."

"Okay, that's enough."

"Sorry."

"That's okay."

Silence.

"Dizzy Gillespie and Willie Nelson were on. Hank Jones and Norah Jones . . ."

"What, no Tom Jones?"

"I don't think so, at least not yet. All the big stars have been on Marian's show. Even, like, Eartha Kitt and Keith Jarrett."

"Not at the same time, I hope."

"No, I don't think so. That opera singer, Renée Fleming. God, she's gorgeous! She was on the show. And what's his name . . . God, this jet lag is *destroying* my memory—the 'Take Five' guy?

"Dave Brubeck."

"Yeah, that's it. He was on. And now, you. So, you want to go in this next store? Wouldn't it be great to meet Tom Jones? Look! They have lots of pins shaped like butterflies. I love butterflies."

∽

When Marian called me in Germany last month I was so excited I almost dropped the telephone. She had read *Piano Girl* and, having logged eight years playing with her trio at New York City's Hickory House, related to my tales of unruly customers, obnoxious managers, stalkers, perverts, and piano gig mishaps. We talked for almost an hour about music and family and raising kids in Europe. She was hip and funny and genuinely interested in my double life as a musician and mom.

A week after our conversation I received a formal letter from her asking me to be a guest on *Piano Jazz*. I ran my hands over her elegant stationery—how odd it is to receive a real letter these days—and gave it a place of honor in my *Piano Girl* scrapbook. Then, feeling a little sad, I called Marian's home number.

"Thank you so much for the invitation," I said. "But I can't be on your show. I'm not a jazz musician. Not even close."

"Oh, that's okay," she said. "It's all just music. Time for something different. We'll play a few tunes and talk about your book. It will be fun! I can't wait!"

∽

Nina and I arrive at Manhattan Beach studio five minutes before noon. My parents, who have come in from Pittsburgh for the taping, are in the control room. I haven't seen them for almost a year, and it feels odd to have our reunion in front of the technicians. Nina takes charge and introduces me to Shari Hutchinson, the *Piano Jazz* producer. Good producers are efficient and keep things moving along. Great producers have vision. Shari's handshake is firm, her manner respectful and friendly, her voice warm and confident. I can tell she knows her craft.

"Marian will be here in a moment," says Shari. "She's freshening up a bit."

For some reason everyone is eating soup. Mom hugs me and continues chatting with the young man at the mixing board. I think they might be exchanging recipes.

Dad says, "How are you doing? You okay?" He knows I get nervous before important piano events. "Do you need something to eat?"

"No thanks, Dad."

"How about some tea?"

"Okay." He pours the tea for me and hands me a little plastic container of cream. I hand it back to him. He opens it for me. I think this may be a sign. Of what, I don't know. Maybe my chakras are aligning.

I check out the two Baldwin grand pianos sitting side by side behind the glass partition.

"Why don't you check out the piano?" says Shari. "You'll be playing the one on the right. We'll get our levels while you're doing that."

"Sure," I say.

"By the way," Shari says. "Marion is sensitive about pictures, so no photos, please."

"Of course," I say. "I understand. But, uh, you might want to mention this to Nina. She has the camera, and she tends to be shutter happy."

"Will do," says Shari.

I head into the studio. It's so peaceful in here. This might be the first real stillness I've experienced since leaving home—even at their most quiet there's a constant drone on the city's streets. I can see the others behind the glass—they look like silent-movie actors, laughing and pointing at who knows what. I pull the charts out of my backpack and a rope of pink pearls spills onto the floor and makes a big racket. The engineer lifts his head. I can't hear him, but he can obviously hear me. I arrange the charts on the piano and stuff the jewelry back inside the backpack.

I'm a recording rookie compared to my husband and my father, both of whom make a living in the recording studio. For me it's still an adventure. John says a recording is exactly that—a *record* of what a musician sounds like during a particular phase of her life. This soothes me. I don't have to sound better than I am. I would, however, like to avoid sounding worse.

I look into the control room. Busy, busy, busy. I wonder if anyone would notice if I left and returned to Nick's Picks. I put my hands on the keys. The first moments at an unfamiliar piano are always awkward.

The piano is in tune. The action is good. Fine.

The studio door clicks behind me, and there she is.

"Robin!" she says. "It's great to have you here! What were you playing just now? Very nice!" She is wearing a spiffy dark-blue pantsuit and a silky blouse with a bow at the neck. She hugs me.

"It's an honor to meet you," I say. Any woman who has managed to make a living as a musician, especially a jazz musician, blows me away. Marian grew up during a time when female jazz musicians were a rarity. In a way they still are.

Shari stands with her hand on Marian's elbow. She leads her to the piano, helps her get situated, then politely excuses herself. I'm surprised by Marian's physical frailness. Her radio voice has always been so strong, her laughter so robust, that I've been tricked into thinking she's decades younger than her ninety years.

"It takes me a few minutes to get comfortable," she says. "I need to have a hip replacement, but who has time for that? I want to go on tour in the fall. My agent has a nice string of gigs lined up."

"Wow," I say. "It's wonderful you're still touring so much."

"Yes!" she says. "Things are good."

We sit on our individual piano benches, our bodies turned to face each other while we're taping the interview sections of the program.

I hand Marian the charts I've brought with me.

"Oh!" she says, tossing the music onto the table between us. "These mean nothing to me. Never did care much for reading notes! I play by ear. Let's figure out what songs we should do as a duet and what key, and off we'll go."

I'm a little thrown by this, since I've spent weeks preparing these arrangements. But it's her show, so I put the charts away and grab a pencil. Together we decide who takes which chorus for each of the songs. I'm scribbling notes, but she doesn't write down a thing.

"Trust me," she says. "This will work out. I hate planning too much."

"Maybe that's the secret to a happy life," I say.

"Might be," she says. "It works for me."

I vow that my next fifty years will be more spontaneous.

"Let's try a chorus of 'Night and Day,'" she says. "I'll play the melody on the head." She turns and faces the piano. And then, before my eyes, this sweet English rose of a grandmother turns into a jazz cat. Get down, Marian. "One, two, one, two three, four . . ."

We play a couple of choruses. I'm having fun.

"Good!" she says. "But let's not rehearse too much."

"You know, Marian," I say. "This is tricky for me. I'm used to playing solo. It's pretty much all I've ever done."

"Well then, these duets will be a premiere!"

"Yeah. Hell of a way to try something for the first time." We both laugh.

"Excuse me, ladies," says Shari from the control room. "Please save the chitchat for the actual taping. Right now we're just testing levels, and I don't want to lose spontaneity."

Rehearsal seems to be a bad word in this place.

Marian waves her hand dismissively toward the control room and says, "Okay, okay," but keeps talking to me, asking about John, my kids, my music. By the time we start taping I'm having so much fun I've completely forgotten why I'm here.

Marian conducts the entire show—several hours of taping—without consulting a single note of music or any kind of written prompt about my book. We play three standard tunes together: "Charade," "Spring Can Really Hang You Up the Most," and "Night and Day." I've practiced my two-piano arrangements for months, but Marian, with her ears leading the way, jumps right in and nails each piece on the first take. I play an original solo piece that I've dedicated to her—one that I've been working on for at least six weeks—and she returns the favor by playing a piece for me that she composes on the spot. She plays, I play, we talk and talk, we play together, then repeat the whole cycle with different topics and different tunes. Her joy rubs off on me. Look at her go—here's a ninety-year-old woman playing piano the way she wants to. She has grown into her music and stayed young because of it. She listens, she responds, she encourages the rest of us to keep going. Marian doesn't need magic, luck, or soothing words to keep her plane in the sky, because she's the pilot. If there's a better role model for a musician, I don't know who it is.

We play the last chord of the last song, and Marian says, "Well, *that* was fun!"

Everyone in the control room applauds, and Marian hugs me.

"I think we should take some pictures," she says.

"Oh, that would be great!" I try to get Nina's attention in the control room, but she is flitting about and exchanging business cards with everyone. Marian pulls out a compact and touches up her lipstick. Then she grabs a can of Final Net hair spray and a small brush and cranks her hair. I realize I've forgotten to bring my makeup—it's back at Hotel Wolcott, on the shelf underneath the NBA makeup mirror. I've got a rope of plastic pearls, three rhinestone bangle bracelets, fake emerald earrings and a belt covered in sequins, but no lipstick.

Nina flies through the studio door with her camera and chokes on the hair-spray fumes. Marian keeps spraying.

"Well," says Marian, taking one last look in her compact. "I'm ready for the photos."

"But Marion," says Shari from the control room. "Don't you want to fix your hair?"

"I just did," says Marian, rolling her eyes.

"And it looks fabulous," says Nina, sneezing in the cloud of Final Net.

"Oh, yes, I see now, your hair does look fabulous," says Shari.

"See?" Nina whispers to me. "Hair *always* counts. You want to borrow my hairbrush?"

Shari escorts my parents into the studio and introduces them to Marian. I feel like I'm at a wedding reception. Marian embraces them and has her photo taken with the three of us.

"Well, Bob," she says to my dad. "You should be proud of your daughter. She played her ass off."

"Yes, Marian, she did."

"You played your ass off, too," I say to Marian. Her hand is on my waist, and she gives me a conspiratorial squeeze.

Marian's driver whisks her away, and I stay at the studio to record several solo holiday pieces for an NPR *Piano Jazz* Christmas CD. My piano has slipped out of tune, so I slide over to Marian's. I imagine, just for a moment, what it's like to be her.

Several weeks later I perform a reading and concert in the rotunda at Steinway Hall. Marian, who has her own concert on the same night, sends flowers. FROM ONE PIANO GIRL TO ANOTHER, the card reads. WISH I COULD BE THERE.

Stopping Traffic

It's Valentine's Day, another one of those holidays made popular by greeting-card companies. I'm driving to my lunchtime piano job at Schlosshotel Lerbach and thinking about Hallmark Cards. My sister, Randy, has a bad reaction to any Hallmark store. There's something about the smell of the paper that causes her to have intestinal cramps. She'll pick out a card, and before she even pays for it, she'll have to race to the nearest ladies' room, not always an easy jaunt in an American mega-mall. I have a similar reaction to the smell of auto-supply stores, but I think that's fairly common among women.

For me, Valentine's Day conjures elementary-school memories of shoe boxes decorated with tinfoil, pastel-colored ribbons, and paper doilies; lacy cards with dopey-looking angels and chubby cupids; and suspicious sentiments printed on dime-sized pieces of heart-shaped candy. BE MINE. LOVE YOU. YOU'RE SWEET. FOREVER YOURS.

I've always worked on Valentine's Day, just like I've always worked on Mother's Day, Christmas, New Year's Eve, and just about every other major secular and religious holiday. I don't complain. I show up and play the piano, happy to have the work, even happier that I don't have to sit around at home waiting for presents and cards bought at stores that cause lower-tract distress.

Today I've dug my red gown out of the back of my closet and squeezed myself into it. I'm grateful it still fits. I don't usually wear red, and I usually don't wear full-length gowns at lunchtime, but if there's a holiday that calls for excess, it's this one. I've been told the brasserie at the castle is fully booked.

As usual I've left the house with just enough time to get to Lerbach. I can make it from my front door to the piano bench in exactly twenty-six minutes, as long as there are no traffic disruptions. I'm listening to Lang Lang play a Chopin nocturne on a Valentine's Day radio program called *Classics for Lovers*. I've turned on my GPS system to see what Kate has to say about the route I've been driving for the past eight years. Maybe she knows a shortcut.

Traffic disruption ahead! Caution. Traffic disruption ahead! Kate sounds a little out of sorts. Her boyfriend probably gave her a Dust Buster as a Valentine's Day gift. And what kind of traffic disruption could there be? I'm on a two-lane highway that winds through a nature reserve. I've run into parades and flea markets in some of the villages, but here?

Traffic disruption! says Kate. I'm about to turn her off when I round the bend and see two riderless horses coming toward me. Side by side, they amble right down the center of the road. A dozen cars creep along behind the horses, waiting for a chance to pass.

There's something sad about the horses. They're wearing saddles and they seem confused or lost. But I don't know, maybe they're happy. With horses it's so hard to tell. Maybe they're thinking, *Let's make a run for it—it's our only chance!* Why isn't anyone doing anything? Surely someone will help. A man in the car behind the horses honks his horn, which seems like a bad idea. The horses look frightened.

Searching for an alternate route, says Kate. But it's too late to turn around.

I pull to the side of the road. With Lang Lang still emoting from the radio, I get out of the car. My gown has one of those extra-long skirts with a small train attached to it. It looks good at the piano, but it's a pain to walk in, especially on asphalt. The shoes aren't helping. I make that *kiss-kiss* noise that works on most animals, and the horses allow me to approach them.

From the car they appeared manageable, but up close they're huge. They're chestnut brown with white faces, pointed ears, and twitching hooves. They check me out and do not look pleased. Unlike my daughter, I don't have the best track record with large animals. Maybe they don't like my gown. I wonder if horses react to red the way bulls do.

Kiss-kiss. Now what? Reins. Think reins. I let go of my skirt and grab the reins of each horse.

Kiss-kiss.

Shit. The horses turn sideways and block both lanes of traffic. The first horse is starting to back up into the other horse, whose nostrils are doing that thing that makes him look like the problem animal in *The Horse Whisperer*. The honking man hits the horn again. I try to channel Robert Redford.

"Okay, boys," I say to the horses. "Help me out here." *Kiss-kiss.*

It works. They calm down. I tug on the reins and lead the horses toward the side of the road. One of them steps on the tail of my skirt. I'm wearing red velvet backless shoes, and I lose one of them when I stumble. I can't reach down to pick it up without letting go of the reins, so I keep going, one shoe off, one shoe on, *kiss-kissing* my way to the curb.

Good. We've reached the side of the road. But I need a plan. I look down at the hoof print on my red gown. I look up at horsey nostrils. I look over my shoulder as the traffic begins to creep by. Dozens of drivers gawk at me as if this entire incident is my fault. I'm shocked that no one offers to help me. Where's that Valentine's Day spirit?

One of the horses chooses this moment to tinkle. I kick my skirt to the side to make sure it's out of harm's way. I decide to let him finish his business before we make our next move.

Wow. That's a lot of tinkle.

Honk-honk. Some people are shaking their heads in disgust, while others are waving and laughing as they drive by.

This is one way to get an audience.

My shoe is in the middle of the road, and two cars in a row drive over it.

"Nice horsies," I say. There's a narrow grassy ridge by the curb and a bike path on the other side of it. If I can get the horses onto the bike path, they'll at least be away from the automobile traffic.

Kiss-kiss. I slide out of my other shoe—if there's anything worse than walking in high heels, it's walking in one high heel—and we climb over the little hill that's between us and the bike path.

"Come on, boys, you can do it," I say. They get ahead of me and pull me over the ridge with them. At last we're on the bike path. I look back at the highway, where my Mazda sits with the door open. The radio is blasting away—Lang Lang is now playing a Rachmaninoff piano concerto. Note to self: Rachmaninoff is way too frantic for Valentine's Day. The other vehicles scoot around my car. My poor shoe. In Germany we have insurance for just about everything. I wonder if I'll be able to file a claim for one shoe.

Should I just release the horses on the bike path and hope for the best? I wonder what time it is. I will surely be late for work. Now what? I'm standing barefoot on a bike path in a red evening gown at high noon with two very large horses looking at me as if I have all the answers. I'll bet even Hallmark doesn't have a card for this.

The lyrics to "Beast of Burden" run through my mind. I spot a pole about 100 meters down the bike path. It might be good enough for a hitching post.

"Okay, fellows, let's go." They trust me. Off we plod toward the pole. Once we get there I throw the reins over the wooden post, which is chest height and painted black and white.

"*Stay*," I say. I'm aware that neither of these animals understands English, but I'm certain if I switch to German the confidence will seep out of my voice and the horses, sensing my panic, will take off at a gallop and drag me back into the middle of the road. I pat them on their very soft noses and wish them luck. Then I head back up the bike path toward my car. I'm shocked to notice how cold it is. Freezing, in fact.

I pick up the shoe I had kicked off by the side of the road and watch as the cars, one by one, continue to run over the other shoe, which lies squashed—Piano Girl roadkill—in the middle of the highway. Finally there's a lull in the traffic, so I look both ways, grab my flattened shoe, and jump back into my car. My feet are numb and I can hardly feel the gas and brake pedals.

Drive straight ahead, says Kate. *The traffic obstruction has been eliminated.*

I'll say. I turn off Lang Lang, turn off Kate, crank the heater, and drive up the road to the spot where I've tied up the horses. I roll down the window and go *kiss-kiss*. The horses are together; they'll be fine. They look, I don't know, *settled*. The car behind me honks. As I pull away, I spot two puzzled-looking young women in riding clothes emerging from the forest, holding hands and racing toward the animals.

∽

Luckily I have my spare gold dress-up sandals in the back of the car, so I won't have to play for a three-course champagne lunch barefoot, not that anyone would care. My coworkers are so busy they don't even notice I'm late, nor do they see the hoof print on my evening gown. I start, of course, with "My Funny Valentine," even though most of my audience won't recognize the song. But what can I do? It's a seasonal piece and it's now or never.

"You okay, Robin?" asks Herr Schröder, the manager. "You look a little stressed."

"Horse," I say.

"Herr Schröder!" says a waiter. "The Northcott-Sampson party has just arrived."

"Did you say *horse?*" he asks me.

"Horses, actually. Two of them."

"Hold on a second," he says, and rushes off to greet the Northcott-Sampsons.

I swivel around on my piano bench to face the restaurant crowd and see lots of middle-aged couples—women with cotton-candy hair drinking rosé champagne, accompanied by men with thinning hair who are also drinking rosé champagne but would rather be drinking beer. Several senior couples top off the crowd, including Frau and Herr Severins, who are in their eighties and manage to show up at the castle once a month. For them, each day really is

Valentine's Day. They've coordinated their outfits to suit the occasion. She is wearing a red silky dress. He has on a red tie.

I've almost forgotten about the horses. We're coasting along at a relaxed champagne-lunch tempo when the manager tells me that Buttercup Blondeau, a well-known porn queen, will be joining us at any moment.

"For lunch?" I say.

"What else?" says Herr Schröder.

Buttercup (possibly not her real name) is one of those porn stars on the radar of most mainstream German citizens. A crossover artist in the truest sense, she has broken away from pure porn and appears regularly as a hostess on a popular television program about *love, love, love*. She shows up in tabloids, society magazines, at fancy parties, and political events. She's a porn-industry success story—a cultural icon.

"*On Valentine's Day?* She's coming here on Valentine's Day?" I ask. I know there's something's wrong with this, but I can't figure out what.

I'm playing "All the Things You Are."

"She's coming with a date," says Herr Schröder. "She's in love. What, just because she's a porn star she's not allowed to be in love? *Au contraire*. Look! He arranged to have a rose waiting for her on the table. Let me tell you, he's one lucky guy!" I glance at the one empty table in the restaurant.

"Here she is now," says Herr Schröder.

Well. Buttercup Blondeau, ready for her close-up, poses in the restaurant's entrance like she's waiting for the waiters to carry her to her table. If she stands there a second longer, I'm sure they'll comply. Ms. Blondeau, who has the most extreme body imaginable—water-balloon breasts and a waist the circumference of a coffee cup—has been decanted into a black cashmere minidress. It's a good dress, an expensive dress, but there's no hiding the real Buttercup. Her makeup looks classy, but she has porn-queen bed-head platinum hair and big puffy lips. I try, really I do, not to think about those lips.

"Have you ever seen one of her films?" I ask Herr Schröder.

"Who, me?" he says. He rushes to greet Ms. Blondeau.

I hold my breath as she enters the room and realize that I'm playing the *Lion King* song "Can You Feel the Love Tonight?" A tune from a Disney movie probably isn't the best entrance music for a film star whose recent releases include classics like *Pass the Butter*, *Dodgeballs*, and *Bride of Spankenstein*, but I continue play-ing. Everything around me shifts into silent mode. At Schlosshotel Lerbach I've played for European queens and Arabian princesses, Brazilian football players, and American film stars. But Buttercup is the first celebrity to bring the castle to a complete standstill. Wow.

I don't even hear a fork clink on a plate. The men stare at Buttercup. The women glare at the men. Buttercup's date, a hand-some manboy with broad shoulders and biceps bulging through his suit coat, follows behind her. Right before she slides into her seat, he kisses her—I mean *seriously* kisses her—while grabbing her ample derriere. I'm playing in the key of D, and I hit an A-flat instead of an A-natural, the ultimate wrong note.

Herr Schröder looks at me and raises one eyebrow.

Gradually, after Buttercup sits down and crosses her very long legs—a spectacle that causes gasping at a nearby table—things return to normal. The guests eat and drink and chat, but I know they're sneaking glances at Buttercup. Heck, I'm doing it myself. You can't *not* look at this woman. I don't know how she can breathe in that dress, or walk in those shoes, or negotiate her way through life with breasts that large. I feel a little sorry for her, but I admire her too. I wonder if she likes music or if she enjoys reading. I wonder about her hobbies. Gardening? Scrabble? Twister?

I begin playing "A Time for Us," the theme from that sixties *Romeo and Juliet* movie.

An apprentice waiter, probably the same age as Buttercup's date, walks past her table, steals a look at her, trips over his own feet, and almost drops a tray of empty wine glasses. The glasses clink together and wobble, but nothing breaks.

Love songs, love songs, nothing but love songs. My thoughts drift back to the horses. I hope they're okay. I wonder if Buttercup is kind to animals. I'd like to see her leading a horse down a highway in those shoes.

I play "Wave."

Later, Buttercup and her date get up to visit the dessert buffet, just as Herr and Frau Severins are leaving. *"Auf Wiedersehen,* Frau Goldsby!" says Frau Severins as she passes the piano. She bends down and whispers in my ear, "Interesting crowd you have here today."

I start to answer but Frau Severins is now focused on her husband. He's staring—open-mouthed—as Buttercup and the date make out like teenagers right in front of the dessert table. The date grabs Buttercup's bottom again—who can blame him?—as she leans over, dangerously close to spilling body parts into the crème brulée. Not that I've ever watched a porn film—who, me?—but I can imagine this looks a lot like the beginning of a scene straight out of *Buttercup Boffs Bielefeld.*

Frau Severins grabs her husband's arm and hauls him out of the brasserie. Buttercup and her date, still hot and bothered, dish out their desserts and sashay back to their table for two, all the while groping and gushing and making goo-goo sounds at each other.

Lunch is over. Usually on an occasion like this, guests linger over coffee and sweets. But today there's a Buttercup-induced mass exodus. The other women in the restaurant, tired of competing for attention with an authentic pornography princess, wrangle their men and lead them to the safety zone—away from the crème brulée, away from the booze, the breasts, the eye candy, and the fun. As they're perp-walked out of the brasserie, the men remind me of the horses. They're a little happy that someone has taken the reins and a little sad to be reminded of where they belong.

Buttercup makes a solo pass by the dessert buffet for a plate of berries and cream. When she gets to the piano she stops and smiles at me. She's older than I thought, maybe even my age.

"Thank you for your lovely music," she says. "I can only imagine how hard it is to play for people who aren't always listening. But you really made this day special for my friend and me. I love that Disney song you played when I came in—I'm a huge Disney fan."

"Thank you," I respond. "Sorry about that wrong note."

"Oh, that's okay," she says. "It's not always easy being an artist."

"That's the truth," I say. I guess she would know. "It's so nice that you could come today—I mean that you could show up and eat—I mean . . . it's so nice to meet you. Thank you for being here, and I wish you a wonderful Valentine's Day."

She smiles, fluffs her hair, and says, "Same to you."

I play "Beauty and the Beast" and call it a day.

The Dancing Drummer

I love a parade. When I was a little girl I logged countless hours sitting on the curb and waiting for my father to march by. My brother, sister, and I perched across the street from the reviewing stand and cheered as high-school bands with a wide range of musical and marching expertise stomped past us. The kids from the rich white schools—in their spotless white uniforms and white military hats with green or purple or red plumes—played arrangements of "You're a Grand Old Flag," "She'll Be Comin' Round the Mountain," and "You Are My Sunshine." With brass instruments reflecting the steely Pittsburgh sky, they moved in perfect formation, no one out of step, each row as straight as a paper edge, squinting at their music.

The military precision of the white bands impressed us, but we preferred the groups from the black high schools. Dressed in ragtag uniforms and playing instruments that might have fallen off a truck, they played their hearts out and packed a wallop as powerful as anything I had ever heard. As they shuffled past us, performing songs like "I Heard It Through the Grapevine" and "Respect," I could feel the sidewalk throbbing along with the bass drum.

"Yeah," my brother would say. "Yeah."

Then there were the dancing girls. The rich kids always had majorettes who twirled batons and a drill team that shook pom-poms. As regimented as the musicians, they marched along with big frozen smiles and even bigger frozen hair, led by a head majorette with a silver whistle and extra sparkles on her uniform. Part of me envied the majorettes. I knew it would be cooler to be *in* the band rather than dancing in front of it, but still, I loved the sequins.

My sister and I were amused by the majorette mothers, a pushy group of middle-aged moms who marched next to their daughters, supposedly protecting them from the perverts lurking along the downtown Pittsburgh parade route. Grim-faced women who wore sleeveless polyester shells and matching stretch pants, they always seemed a little surprised to be where they were, as if their own parades had passed them by sooner than expected.

Sometimes the black bands had a couple of dancing girls, but they were way too hip to have any majorette mothers.

"That's the school I'm going to when I grow up," my sister said. "Any place with an anti-majorette policy is fine with me."

"That poor girl in the back is missing a tooth," my mother said, her eyes welling with tears. Mom noticed things like that. She had an eagle eye for unfortunate children, spotting the frayed hemline, the taped glasses, the lunch-stained uniform. Presented with any group of kids, black or white, rich or poor, she could point out the teenager having a hard time at home. This made it tricky for her to truly enjoy a parade, because every group of youngsters included a boy in the saxophone section with the wrong color pants or an earnest fourteen-year-old clarinet player with bad skin and a featherless hat, marching forward one step at a time and hoping to make it to the end of the route without anyone laughing. Or in Mom's case, crying.

Sooner or later the Musicians Union Trust Fund Band—an aging group of white guys—would approach the reviewing stand.

Dressed in black caps, navy-blue blazers, and gray slacks—the working musician's Confederate Army costume—they coasted through the music, even though most of them had stayed out late the night before working in jazz joints, nightclubs, and burlesque theaters. Strolling along Fifth Avenue they offered effortless performances of songs like "Stars and Stripes Forever" and "God Bless America." Sometimes Dad played bass drum, sometimes snare, sometimes cymbals. He always sounded great.

The union band never had majorettes—they didn't have the budget to spend money on babes in short skirts, at least not while marching—but they had Dad to keep the crowd entertained. At each parade I held my breath and leaned forward on the curb, hoping to see him coming, knowing he was bound to think of something silly, a prank or two for our amusement. He marched backwards, he tap-danced, he wore an Indian headdress or a hula skirt or a Frankenstein mask; he once marched the second half of the parade route while wearing a duck costume, never missing a beat.

Dad set a record at one county fair celebration by taking three jobs in one parade, all of them with Trust Fund bands. In the sixties the parade scale for a professional musician was around eighteen dollars, not much for a drummer with a family of five. But three jobs in one parade? That worked out to a pretty good payday. The union bands were staggered throughout the parade, one at the beginning, one in the middle, and one at the end. Because Dad didn't want to worry about switching instruments, he arranged to play cymbals in all three bands. He layered his uniforms and fixed a ride in a cop's motorcycle sidecar to rush from the end of the parade route back to the start. The crowd sat on wooden bleachers and watched as three versions of Dad marched by—making a living, making music, making everyone laugh.

One year at the end of a July Fourth celebration, Nick Parillo, the bandleader on many of the Trust Fund parade gigs, insisted on leading the band through the *1812 Overture*, the much-played Tchaikovsky composition that calls for a volley of cannon fire at the end. Nick, without telling the musicians, had talked four VFW guys—all of whom had spent the morning at a local bar—into hiding in trees with their rifles. The dramatic conclusion to the *1812 Overture* sounded more like the first day of hunting season. The shooters, none of whom had a clue about rhythm, fired random blanks, leaving the musicians running for cover and poor Nick madly waving his baton at the trees.

The spectacle of those parades, the memory of those butt-numbing three-hour waits on a cold piece of concrete, have stayed with me all these years. I can still hear the cool cadence of the Westinghouse High School drum line, the swish of the pom-poms, and the Mt. Lebanon head majorette's whistle. I can see thousands of white-booted feet pounding past us, the swirling colors of the twirling flags, and my father dancing down the avenue for his children, as if the entire parade were meant solely for us.

I had way more fun watching parades than I did marching in them. I had started playing the flute in the first grade. Every year on Independence Day, as a penalty for playing an instrument that resembled a fife, I had to don a Revolutionary War outfit and march around Chatham Village—a National Landmark community in the Mt. Washington section of Pittsburgh—playing endless choruses of "Yankee Doodle Dandy." My little brother, Curtis, played the parade drum, and my sister, Randy, whose talents fell outside the music field, posed as a wounded soldier, with a ketchup-smeared bandage wrapped around her head. She limped along beside us on one crutch, looking as pathetic as possible, while waving a torn American flag with her free hand. Randy got all the attention, especially once we added "When Johnny Comes Marching Home" to our repertoire. Through the village we marched—covering Pennridge, Olympia, Bigham, and Sulgrave Roads—rousing residents with my brother's uneven drum cadence, my own piercing flute lines, and the *clump-clump* of my sister's crutch on the asphalt. The adults waved and took photos, the smaller children followed along behind us, and the older kids waited until we rounded the corner and laughed. I can still hear them.

There's not a teenager this side of Williamsburg who would be caught dead in a three-cornered hat, and I was no exception. At fifteen I staged a protest and stopped marching in the Chatham Village parade. This meant the end of our child-soldier band, because what's a fife-and-drum corps without the fife?

But I didn't give up on parades. We had a long tradition of parade participants in our family, and I was determined to do my part. So I began playing in the South Hills High School Marching Band. No hats. Plus we had a cool bandleader named Mr. Lansberry and the distinction of being a public high school with a solid mix of black and white students. Marching-band arrangements included songs we were hearing on the radio, and, against my better judgment, I found myself playing piccolo on tunes like "Smoke on the Water" and the theme from *The Exorcist*. I hated that damn piccolo. It didn't weigh much, but still. I truly believed it capable of inducing seizures, provoking migraines, and attracting rabid dogs.

Mr. Lansberry, who knew I had a good sense of rhythm—I was, after all, the drummer's daughter—saw I was suffering in the piccolo line and promoted me to cymbals. Dad taught me some nifty twirling tricks, and I was ready to go. I enjoyed the cymbals, maybe a little too much. The local news got some footage of me bashing away in a Columbus Day parade, and, much to my embarrassment, incorporated the segment into their nightly news trailer. For years I was on the evening news, earnestly slamming my cymbals together as we played our rocking version of "Spinning Wheel."

Eventually I decided I was too cool for the marching band and opted to join the cheerleading squad. It was hardly a dignified substitute for music, but the outfits were flashier, the pom-pom dances were fun, and the boys paid more attention. Plus there were more black girls on the cheerleading squad than in the marching band. We were swingin'. My sister, who had long ago discarded her Revolutionary War bandage and crutch, inherited my cymbals and my place in the drum line. She used to sneak up behind the cheerleaders, the majorettes, and their mothers, crash the cymbals together as loudly as she could, and scare the spangles off all of us.

᭤

Being stuck in a parade is very different from marching in one. My own personal parade led me to New York City, where there's a parade or two every single day. Christopher Street Parade! Macy's Thanksgiving Day Parade! St. Patrick's Day Parade! But the famous parades, both gorgeous and grand, couldn't compare to the Puerto Rican Day Parade and the joy and chaos it created in Midtown Manhattan. I played the piano Sundays in various Manhattan hotels, usually starting at noon. On most weekend mornings the traffic was lazy, and I could grab coffee to go, hail a cab, and make it to my brunch gig with little effort. But every year those Puerto Ricans ambushed me. *Wham!* Parade time, like it or not.

There I would sit, trapped in Midtown with a cursing cab driver, blaring horns, and women outfitted in red spandex diaper pants spinning round and round and shaking their behinds to deafening salsa music. Getting out of the cab to walk wasn't any better. Flag wavers and screaming teenagers jammed the sidewalks. Breaking through the crowd meant shoving, apologizing, cussing, and climbing over barricades. I would emerge on the other side of the parade, right on the border of Times Square, disheveled, out of breath, and late for work.

᷉

The New York City Marathon is the finest kind of parade, mainly because it's ambitious and high-speed. No dancing girls, majorette mothers, twirling cymbals, or feathered hats—just 40,000-plus runners dashing through the five boroughs, each of them focused on a distant goal. In the fifteen years I lived and worked in New York City I almost always found myself on the elevated subway platform at Queensboro Plaza on Marathon Sunday, staring down at the column of runners headed onto the ramp of the Fifty-ninth Street Bridge. I might have enjoyed the spectacle, but—*here comes Mom*—my eyes would roam to the runner who limped, the man with the tattered running clothes, or the sad-looking woman with the pink T-shirt that read "THIS IS FOR YOU, AUNT BETSY." I'd start to cry, then rush to my Sunday brunch piano job with swollen eyes and a runny nose.

In 1991, determined to avoid another Marathon meltdown, I left two hours early for work, thinking I could avoid the race. As was my habit, I changed trains at Queensboro Plaza. I looked down—expecting to see an empty roadway—but there they were: The wheelchair runners; the blind runners; the runners with one leg, or no legs, or no arms; the mentally challenged runners; runners pulling each other up the ramp to the bridge, crossing the East River and creeping—in some cases crawling—toward the finish line.

An older man wearing light blue shorts and dark wraparound sunglasses jogged along with his hand balanced on the forearm of a young woman. She was his "sighted runner," guiding him through the race. Was she a friend or a relative? Or was she a volunteer, a trained marathon runner willing to go the distance just to share this man's joy when he crossed the finish line? Was she leading him or was he leading her? I watched until they disappeared into the crowd, feeling both inspired and aimless, as if I could conquer the world if I had a sighted runner of my own.

Later that day, when I described the blind runner to a friend of mine, he asked: "How did he know when to turn? Did someone stand on the corner and shout *make a right?*"

"No," I said. "The blind man allowed the sighted woman to guide him. He, well, he just trusted her." I couldn't talk about this without breaking into tears.

৸৽

"How can you move to Germany?" a friend of mine once asked. "Considering the history, it seems like a pretty scary place."

A few months before we moved we traveled to New Hope, Pennsylvania, a popular riverside resort ninety minutes from New York City, known for its artist colony and unhurried pace. John was scheduled to play a concert there, so baby Curtis and I went with him, unaware that more than 2,000 neo-Nazis would be arriving and marching through the gay-friendly town on the same day. We watched as the buses pulled into a large parking lot on the edge of the quaint city center. Men and women—hatemongers from distant towns—jumped off the buses, looking for trouble. Their boots were thick and black, their heads shaved, their tattoos angry and sad. We moved far away, trying to entertain our son by feeding ducks in a nearby park, but the sound of their stomping boots and the drone of their ugly chanting, insistent and familiar in an eerie way, ruined the day. I knew that groups like this existed in the United States, but I had never run into one.

"Germany? Aren't you concerned about the neo-Nazis?" asked another American friend.

To this day, the only neo-Nazis I've come across were in New Hope, Pennsylvania. I guess some people fail to see the parade, especially when it's hateful and deadly and marching right past them.

∽

When we first moved to Germany we lived in a little village called Donrath, a *Dorf* where children play outside and ride bikes. In Donrath I hardly ran into anyone speaking English, let alone a Puerto Rican Day, St. Patrick's Day, or Columbus Day celebration. I didn't reckon with *Erntedankfest*, which celebrates the harvest and gives farmers a chance to show gratitude for their crops.

"Good grief!" said my husband as he opened the shutters at ten in the morning. There, not two meters from our bedroom window, sat a tractor-drawn wagon with a load of elderly women singing and knocking back tiny glasses of schnapps. Quite jolly and very tipsy, they beckoned us outside, where they presented us with little bouquets of dried flowers, paper cups filled with potato salad, and schnapps strong enough to blow our heads off.

"Get ready!" they shouted. "The *Erntedankfest* parade is about to begin!"

"Wow, check this out!" John pointed down the street at the long line of floats and tractors. I could hear a glockenspiel—the only instrument more annoying than the piccolo—warming up. We fetched Curtis, two years old at the time, strapped him in his buggy, walked down a little stretch of pavement called *In der Falmerswiese* (in Falmer's field), and waited for the start of our first parade in Germany. Our neighbors, regulars at the annual *Erntedankfest* parade, looked happy to be there, but a little bored.

"It's nice for the kids," Herr Wisgen said. "They like to catch the candy." Herr Wisgen didn't have any children, but there he stood, plastic sack at the ready, looking a bit like an eight-year-old boy on Christmas morning.

I glanced at Herr Wisgen, looked at my son in his plaid coat and wool cap, took in the small crowd of neighbors gathered on the side of the street. I heard the drums start to play, and an unexpected longing for home grabbed hold of me.

"Are you okay?" asked John.

"I'm fine," I said, wiping my eyes. "It's just the drums."

"Oh," said John.

"Drums!" shouted Curtis.

"Look!" said Herr Wisgen. "Here comes the parade!"

First an ambulance drove by. Not a good sign. But then the fun began.

"Look at that," John said. "The Cheese Float." Girls wearing white bonnets passed wedges of soft cheese and crackers to the spectators. A plaster cow balanced on the back of the tractor.

"And here comes the Goat Man." Dressed in *Lederhosen* and sporting a chest-length beard and a felt hat with a feather, the Goat Man, who accompanied three goats on leashes, strolled along and waved. He seemed very authentic. His outfit reminded me of one of Dad's costumes.

Curtis pointed at the goat and said, "Sheep!"

"Goat!" I said.

"Sheep," said Curtis, who was already learning to argue.

"Look! It's the Wheat Float." Boys in overalls gave us little squares of *Schwarzbrot* smeared with butter. I chased the float and had seconds.

Next up was a wagon of men drinking beer and singing. They did not give us beer but threw hard candy at our feet.

"Don't eat that," said a well-meaning neighbor. "It's left over from last year's *Karneval* parade."

"Bon-bombs!" said Curtis.

Herr Wisgen grabbed the candy and put it in his sack.

At last, a real live band! The group featured eight glockenspiels, a couple of trumpets, and three drummers. Out of step and out of tune, they marched along behind a drum major with a spongy face who conducted the band with the gravity of a man leading a presidential funeral procession.

"Scary," said Curtis.

"That baton looks like a baseball bat," said John, as the drum major waved his baton back and forth like he was holding a sorcerer's wand. "I wonder where 'one' is."

The *Funkenmariechen*, dancing girls wearing bright red skirts, white blouses, and—could it be?—three-cornered hats, followed along behind the band. Not one of them smiled. For a moment the drum major, the band, and the *Funkenmariechen* were all performing in different rhythms. It was almost hip, but not quite.

"Look!" said John. "Forget the band. Here comes the Apple Float."

"Apple!" said Curtis. A giant cardboard apple, strapped to the front of a tractor, rumbled toward us. Next to it marched the Apple Ladies, wearing ruffled aprons and large straw hats with wide brims. They carried apples in their apron pockets and paring knives in their hands. They scooted to the sidewalk and cut wedges of fruit for us.

Next came the Egg Float, featuring a man dressed as a chicken. Curtis screamed—with good reason—when he saw the chicken man, but he calmed down when a basket-toting girl handed us dyed eggs. Her colleague stood by with a bottle, pouring *Eierlikör*, the ingredients of which include raw eggs and schnapps, whipped together and aged for several years.

"Now I know what the ambulance is for," said John.

"Meat, mo' meat!" said Curtis, who was stuffing a piece of *Fleischwurst* into his mouth. "Mo' meat!"

"Oh my God," I said, horrified, as I watched my vegetarian son scarf down something that looked like a giant slice of bologna. "Where did he get that?"

"Mo' meat," Curtis said. "Mo' meat."

"It's the Meat Float!" said John.

"'Mo' meat!"

"Hey, this stuff is good," said John.

"Don't eat that!" I said.

"Listen," said John. "I'm a jazz musician. No way I'm going to turn down free food."

I reached for another drink, one without raw eggs in it.

We filled our sacks with candy and flowers and little bottles of mystery alcohol and meat. We clapped for the second group of dancing girls, who seemed happier, possibly because they weren't wearing three-cornered hats. The second band came by and played raucous Cologne *Karneval* music. Another ambulance cruised past us, looking for fallen spectators. The parade was over. We went home and took very long naps.

∽

During *Karneval* Europeans flock to Cologne to watch the annual *Rosenmontag* parade. It's the German version of the Macy's parade, with bands and floats and various *Karneval* organizations competing for slots in the program. But unlike the Macy's event, the spectators also wear costumes, making it difficult to tell the parade participants from the audience. The route is lined with groups of adults dressed in matching kangaroo costumes, clusters of clowns clutching ratty cloth sacks for collecting candy, and muscular men in pink ballerina tutus.

The *Rosenmontag* parade is fun for kids—who could deny the charm of a giant costume party with free candy?—but the drinking sometimes gets out of hand, spreading beyond the parade route to those of us who—in spite of the closed shops and forced cheer—just want to have a normal Monday afternoon. Like Puerto Rican Day in New York City, *Rosenmontag* takes over. It owns the day.

My friend Andrea Hall refused to attend the parade last year and instead went to an indoor swimming pool, where a *Karneval*-crazed teenager slammed into her at the bottom of a giant slide. She lost consciousness and woke up in an emergency room next to dozens of hungover clowns, retching wenches, and wizards with broken limbs. The nurse who treated her was wearing an orange Bozo wig and a red clown nose.

∽

Saint Martin's Day pays tribute to a Roman soldier who saw the error of his Roman ways and became a monk. Legend has it that one night in the middle of a snowstorm Saint Martin—not to be confused with Steve Martin—gave half of his coat to a beggar. I'm not sure how this event qualified Martin for sainthood or why we have a parade in his name, but every year around the eleventh of November, Germany's children march through the streets with handmade paper lanterns singing about Saint Martin and his coat.

The kids here might grow up celebrating *Martinstag*, but I experienced the holiday for the first time as a parent. After a kindergarten craft-session miscommunication that resulted in me hot-gluing the knees of my Donna Karan tights together, I proudly presented my son with a paper lantern that looked just like an owl. We braved the biting November wind and marched with other children and their parents behind a white horse that carried a woman dressed as Martin, which added a nice Christopher Street twist to the celebration. Kids sang at the top of their lungs—endless verses about Martin and his coat—and the adults marched along, trying to ignore the cold. At the end of the parade we gathered around a bonfire and the children were given huge sweet *Brötchen* shaped like puffy men.

This seemed to be a lot of fuss about a guy—saint or not—who gave away only *half* of his coat. Maybe the standards for sainthood were lower in those days. None of it made sense to me, but for years I marched alongside my kids—a majorette mother in a down parka—encouraging them to hold their handmade lanterns high, to stay away from the horse droppings and the bonfire, to sing out, and to remember to leave their coats on, no matter what the legend said.

We once visited Paris on a blustery day in April. With Curtis and his little sister, Julia, in tow, we set out to show them the sights, hoping they might absorb some of the city's light and culture. We visited the *Jardin des Enfants*, ate lunch next to a pond in the *Jardin des Tuilleries*, and headed to *l'Arc de Triomphe* because Curtis wanted to see it. I had visited *l'Arc* once before, in 1977, with my college roommate Deb. Deb almost caused an international incident when—trying to snap a photo of me—she backed up for a better shot and stepped on the Tomb of the Unknown Soldier, an accident that would have gone unnoticed had she not been wearing red cowboy boots with five-inch stiletto heels that got stuck in the cracks of the pavement. She apologized again and again to the *gendarme* who helped extract her from the crack. Thankfully, he did not throw us both in *la prison*. Deb and I, humiliated and a little shaken, walked to the other side of the monument. There, with dark blue uniforms and proud faces, stood a group of French World War II veterans, perhaps a hundred of them, preparing to march around *l'Arc de Triomphe* in an annual tribute to their fallen comrades. The drummers played a solemn cadence, and the veterans began marching. We followed along behind them to the Tomb of the Unknown Soldier—the very spot Deb had just trampled. The *gendarme* glared at us.

Twenty-five years later I was back. The flame on *la Tombe* burned blue in the April air. I remembered Deb and her boots, and smiled. That's when I heard the drums.

"Parade?" said Julia. "Let's go see."

We rounded the corner, and there they were, French World War II veterans in blue uniforms, but this time only twenty or so of them. The drummer played his cadence; the soldiers began their procession. They moved slowly around *l'Arc*, eyes straight ahead, flags high, some of them struggling to keep up. It occurred to me that every year, for more years than I've been alive, these same men have marched in this April parade. And every year more of them are gone. They had survived not just the war but the parade of time, and they were duty bound, by tradition or honor or love, to keep marching.

Like time, a parade moves forward, headed nowhere in particular. I've chased candy and waved to grown men dressed as *Karneval* kangaroos; I've applauded veterans and sung songs about half-coated saints. I've accepted food from bearers of apples and cheese, and I've tried to ignore the sound of stomping black boots crushing new hope and old. I've cheered for marathon runners and cringed at majorette mothers; I've felt ashamed for the boy with the mismatched socks and envied the girl with the crutch and the ketchup-covered bandage. I've marched. I've watched. Watching is better.

Now I stand shoulder to shoulder with my children. I tell them stories from my personal parade history and how their grandfather kept us laughing while their grandmother cried over children in shabby uniforms. We hear the music. Together, we crane our necks and look up the street to see what's coming next. The kids have their own expectations. But I'm waiting for the dancing drummer—the light-footed man who skips sideways through the city streets—to share his joy. He will pause in front of us, bash his cymbals together with a flourish and a twist, and we will understand.

Here comes Mom. There goes Dad.

We're part of the parade, even when we're not.

What to Wear

A middle-aged American woman playing the piano at a castle in Germany has legitimate wardrobe concerns. Most cocktail dresses and evening gowns are designed for chichi events that involve nothing more strenuous than posing in a corner with a tilted head, a shy-sly Princess Di smile, and a fluted champagne glass. They are cut of silk and velvet, feature beaded panels, and often include ruching that slips, slides, and snags if the wearer dares to inhale, laugh, or eat a meatball.

It might look easy, but playing the piano for hours at a time involves an athletic prowess more often associated with trapeze artists and archers. We swing and sway, we remain statue-still while we focus our minds and bodies, we stretch, and we leap without a net when necessary. Imagine one of the Flying Zucchinis performing in high heels and a full-length evening gown with a fishtail skirt and a jewel-encrusted top that chafes her underarms. Treacherous. Or what if William Tell had been forced to shoot that apple from his son's head while an annoying puffed sleeve with seed-pearl embroidery slipped from one shoulder? Poor little Walter would have wound up with an arrow in his thigh. Or worse.

It might be a niche market, but really, someone should come up with a line of gowns for performing female musicians. Something with a little pizzazz, a little Lycra, and a lot of draping.

"Well," says my friend Amy. "Except for the pizzazz part, that would be a burqa." She plays the guitar and has her own wardrobe issues.

I pause for a moment and think about a cocktail pianist wearing a burqa.

"A burqa with bling," I say.

"Perfect," she says.

๏

My Wardrobe: A Brief History

Nantucket

Back in the seventies I loved to dress like Barbie. When I was eighteen I wore tube tops and Dolly Buster halters combined with see-through chiffon skirts so short they had matching panties. They were called Sizzlers. Bad enough to go to school like this, but I was showing up for cocktail piano gigs in these getups. Because I was eighteen and on a budget, I also wore secondhand prom dresses to work—not the prim and proper Little Bo Peep gowns popular with the nice Catholic girls, but hooker-hottie designs intended to make a perfectly healthy teenage pianist look like one of Gangsta Fatboy's groupies ready to take on the band.

I favored one dress—an electric-blue sateen-spandex thing—that was cut down to here and up to there. It threatened to expose my left breast every time I reached for the bass notes. Did this bother me? No. I learned to play while yanking at the bodice of the dress, wondering why five or six drunken sailors crowded around the piano and stuffed money in my tip jar every time I pounded out "I Feel the Earth Move." I lunged for the keys and actually believed

I had a loyal group of seafaring, gin-guzzling, Carole King–loving fans. But now I know it was the blue dress. They yelled for more. I kept going. In a weird way, that dress taught me how to play. So I suppose it was good for something.

I wore frosted lip gloss and a drugstore fragrance called Wind Song by Prince Matchabelli because my high-school boyfriend saved his money and gave me a bottle for graduation. I decided it would be my signature scent. Forever.

Everything is forever when you're eighteen.

∽

New York City: The Early Years

In the eighties I dashed from one Manhattan location to another, covering lunches, cocktail hours, and late-night piano shifts in hotels that catered to tourists wearing swollen white tennis shoes with lightning bolts on the sides. When I got to know a high-class call girl named Jennifer who worked the hotel bar sporting a stretchy blue dress similar to mine, I dropped the Happy Ho look and entered a new era of Piano Girl fashion—a makeover inspired by my newfound ability to buy dresses made by companies other than JCPenney.

I developed a fondness for Betsey Johnson, Calvin Klein, and Isaac Mizrahi. I hardly ever paid retail for these beautiful things—I bought them from a member of the Marriott Marquis housekeeping staff who set up shop in a hotel ladies' room in the toilet stall for the handicapped. She sold her hot-off-the-truck garments by hanging them on rails inside the stall. I shopped at Stall for the Handicapped on my breaks. Maria was a stellar saleswoman, and it was hard to beat the prices.

I remember a bright yellow silk coat I bought from her. It fell to the floor in fragile layers and made me feel like a butterfly when I flitted across the cavernous Marriott lobby. But at the piano the fabric tangled around my elbows and twisted around my knees. I looked like a crumpled piece of birthday-party gift wrap with a head and hands.

Although I hadn't yet succumbed to support hose or underpants with stretchy tummy panels, I did begin to wear a well-constructed bra. *Strap 'em down.* During this phase I began searching for the perfect strapless bra, a mission that continues to this day. Structural engineers know how to hold up multiple floors of a building with one set of well-placed suspension cables, so you'd think they could design a comfortable strapless bra for a pianist. But structural engineers don't have to sit at a Steinway playing arpeggios while wearing an armpit-exposing camisole in a delicate shade of taupe. I doubt that many of them even know what taupe is, which is okay because they have more important tasks.

The thing is, no one forced me to dress this way. It was a choice. I loved dressing up, I loved shopping, I loved leaping out of taxis in my jeans and sneakers and running to the ladies' room with my gig bag strapped over my shoulder. I never carried music or set lists or sound equipment. Instead, I brought along a collapsible evening gown in a festive color—*raspberry! mango!*—and a tissue-thin scarf I could throw over my shoulders when the meat-locker air conditioner kicked on in the middle of my second set. I also carried two pairs of high heels, knowing that my pedal foot would start to ache a few hours into the gig and I would want to change shoes. One pair of golden sandals, purchased on sale at Bergdorf Goodman in 1984, has been with me for twenty-five years. They still hurt. They're still in my gig bag. They are the only things from that part of my life that fit, so I cling to them, thinking they'll march me back to my twenties if I ever need to return. They are the Piano Girl version of Dorothy's ruby slippers, twin metallic talismans that remind me of home.

The accessory pocket of my gig bag held glittery barrettes, rhinestone clips, and sparkly pins and necklaces from Grandma Curtis, all of them offering a pain- and risk-free way to smarten an outfit while reminding me of her. Before she died she had packed all of her costume jewelry in a white cardboard box. "These things are for Robin," her note said. "She's the only one crazy enough to wear them." After she was gone I would play her favorite song—"Theme from Love Story"—and feel the weight of her fake-topaz bracelet circling my wrist. Shalimar was my fragrance. Spicy, flashy, a little too expensive, but very grown-up. Grandma Curtis would have loved it.

∽

New York City: The Final Years

For several years my closet resembled a black hole. I became a reverse negative of myself—blonder hair, darker clothes, skinnier body. I was nobody's trophy wife, but away from the piano I looked the part—half artiste, half social X-ray. I entered my minimalist stage, favoring gowns that didn't deviate from the color palette of, say, a bruise.

New York City was full of paper-thin women in black crepe dresses. I wanted to be one of them and blend into the gallery-going museum-hopping chic-but-trendy kir-sipping crowd—but, with a grand piano in front of me, I never quite fit in. I hid behind my hair and accessorized my outfits with items from Grandma's cardboard box. I discovered her clip earrings with dark stones—polished hunks of jet and deep-blue faux sapphire that suited my wardrobe and my mood.

I wore Chanel No. 5 because it smelled the way I felt. There, but not really. I didn't believe in forever anymore. I tossed the scarves. They were driving me crazy, the way they kept slipping off and falling into fabric puddles at my feet.

I learned to despise hyphenated fashion terms like peep-toe, demi-cup, semi-gloss, push-up, and sling-back when I discovered that all of these things not only looked tacky-tacky, they hurt-hurt. I rearranged my closet, getting rid of anything with ruffles, sequins, bright colors, or feathers. I wanted plain and simple. I wanted people to stop looking and start listening. I wanted loose and light and noncommittal, preferably in a medium-weight silk shantung, with sleeves. I wanted to disappear into a midnight-blue piano mist.

Then I fell in love, an event that called for a new look. I bought an Anna Sui bridal minidress that I could also wear to piano jobs, minus the giant veil. Color returned to my wardrobe. I stopped disappearing and decided it was okay to be both seen and heard.

Forever made a comeback.

ლ

Bergisch Gladbach, Germany

Long before I began playing at Schlosshotel Lerbach, I spotted a ball skirt in the window of the Cologne Laura Ashley store. I dragged my family into the store so I could touch the skirt. Pale pink roses were embroidered on the rich crème silk, and three underlayers of silk and tulle gave the garment a gentle poof. It was the perfect skirt for, say, a lunch date in eighteenth-century Versailles. Not exactly optimal for a day trip to the Cologne Zoo, which was the extent of my social life in the late nineties. I had taken four years off from piano gigs in upscale hotels, opting instead for babies and writing at home. Rewarding, but lonely. My glamorous wardrobe, a size too small and several years out of style, sat in the back of my closet. I claimed not to miss the dress-up routine, but I couldn't explain the sadness I felt whenever I caught sight of all those pretty things, gossamer souvenirs of a past I was happy to have escaped.

In an act of kindness I shall never forget, my husband waited for the end-of-season sale, sneaked back to Laura Ashley, and bought that skirt for me. Two weeks later, the Schlosshotel Lerbach director invited me to play at the castle. It was almost as if he knew I had the right outfit. I wore the skirt, and the maître d', a lovely man named Monsieur Thomann, tossed pink rose petals on the piano. I've been there ever since. I still have the Laura Ashley skirt, along with a large collection of formal dresses purchased on sale over the last decade. They are beautiful things, but decidedly uncomfortable.

My pianist friend Robin Spielberg told me that a grand-piano pedal once ate her ball gown. I never really believed her until it happened to me. The bottom half of a full-length gown can easily become prey to a piano's pedal system. One moment you're fine, the next thing you know—*schwoop!*—you're being sucked into the piano. And the more you pedal, the further in you go. The only choice is to rip the skirt out of the pedal, accept the damage, and soldier on with the music.

The older I get, the more I consider how nice it would be to get away from all of this twisting, pinching, and gapping and wear, say, a bathrobe to work. Or at least a ball gown cut like a bathrobe.

I remember one pianist in New York City—let's call her Sandy—who got in trouble for wearing a Statue of Liberty outfit, complete with headpiece. It was hard to make a bad wardrobe choice in mid-1980s Manhattan, but Sandy's caftan and spiked crown caused a minor uproar with the Marriott management. The other Piano Girls and I laughed at the time. What was she thinking?

Now I wonder if Sandy was on to something. I play at a castle. I could, if I wanted to, wear a tiara, preferably something tasteful with very large emeralds. It would draw attention away from my body, which I could then drape in a velvet cape or an ermine-trimmed robe. I'd wear relaxed-fit pants under the cape, along with an expensive support bra capable of sequestering the twins during those bass-note lunges. So far, my fear of looking like Queen Elizabeth has stopped me from following through on this idea. Even Grandma Curtis, lover of all things sparkling and bright, drew the line at wearing tiaras. Plus my teenage daughter would never talk to me again if I started wearing a crown to work.

Fact: I now spend more money on undergarments than I spend on dresses. Ball gowns, with their nipped waists and tight bodices, require major foundation help. Do not get me started on Spanx, those flesh-colored medieval instruments of torture meant to smooth out the mature figure. Other women swear by them. They make me feel like a stuffed sausage—a very mature stuffed sausage—and that's not a great thing when I'm trying to make music. "If you look good you feel good" does not apply to a fifty-year-old woman who plays the piano for a living. If I feel good, I am probably wearing my Ultimate Pajamas, a sweat suit, or a potato sack. Nobody feels good sitting at the piano in a skintight satin dress with a boned corset—unless, of course, she is eighteen, oblivious to pain, and wearing Wind Song eau de toilette.

Which leaves me with my present-day wardrobe dilemma. Shall I chuck the fancy gear and start dressing like a man? A reliable tuxedo would be a welcome relief after so many years of death by evening gown. I can feel it coming on, another wardrobe make-over—this one, finally, focused on comfort.

Grandma Curtis will continue to provide her glitter-girl accessories. But I shall wear lovely suits in lightweight wool, with loose-fitting pants and non-clinging jackets. I'll select silken blouses in jewel tones and lingerie that's soft and non-constricting.

And the Bergdorf Goodman golden sandals? They will stay in my gig bag, polished and ready to go, just in case I have another change of heart. They'd even look good with a burqa.

The Girl That Got Away

My daughter started riding horses when she was seven years old, the same year she started piano lessons. Julia is twelve now, tall and fit and not quite ready to grow up. Every Monday she spends three hours mucking stalls and brushing the glossy backs of ponies and horses with names like Fury, Flocke, Classic, and Freiheit. A pony named D'Artagnan is her favorite—Darty for short. She picks caked-up straw and manure from Darty's hooves, braids his mane, combs his tail, and whispers who-knows-what into his twitchy ears. She rides through rain and wind and clouds of dust, cantering and trotting and galloping through an uncomplicated childhood.

Darty is sinewy and white. Lina Schwarz, the owner of the stable, rescued him from the clutches of the Zirkus Trampolini family—a small European circus with five performers, including an overweight trapeze artist who sold popcorn at intermission and a fire-eater who doubled as the ticket taker. Darty, I am told, was the animal act. When the circus went bankrupt, Lina snagged him for her riding business. The first time I see Darty with a girl on his back I think he looks like a circus stallion with a death wish—the Charles Bronson of the pony world.

Only the older girls, the more experienced riders, are allowed to ride Darty. He bucks a lot—a comical reverse kick-step—throwing his back legs up and threatening to dump his rider on her head.

The move starts to make sense when you realize his formative years were spent wearing a red feathered hat and running circus-ring laps with a member of the Trampolini family standing on his back. He scares the bejesus out of me, but Julia loves him.

When I was a little girl my sister and I played a game we called Let's Go Die. We rode on each other's bicycle handlebars, stood on our heads for hours at a time, and once tried to do eighteen underwater somersaults in a row while holding onto each other. We were convinced that no matter how we tempted fate, nothing bad would ever happen. I don't hear Julia using the phrase "let's go die," but I know when she's riding Darty she's thinking it. If I were a twelve-year-old with a feisty white horse, this is exactly what I would do. I would ride faster, faster, faster, and make my parents blanch and gasp and cover their eyes. Then I would laugh at them.

As I watch her in action I tumble into a time-jumble machine, one that jostles my sleepy spirit of adventure and spits me out just in time to catch a glimpse of who I used to be. Somewhere in between Let's Go Die, the game of children, and Let's Stay Alive, the game of adults, there's a game called puberty where a kid can play a little of both. That's where Julia is now. Half circus artist, half sophisticated woman of the world, a foreigner in two places at once with a rowdy white pony to catapult her from one side to the other.

⌇

Lina's riding stall is protected by two rottweilers named Honey and Bunny. They don't much like my husband and me, which doesn't suit our Let's Stay Alive philosophy. Every week Honey and Bunny bark and snarl and threaten to tear out our throats. With increasing levels of ferocity they attempt to leap over a chicken-wire fence held together by staples, rubber bands, and string. They don't bark at the other parents. Just us. I decide they don't like my American accent, so I attempt to clean up my German when I'm around them. This makes me sound Swedish. Honey and Bunny bark more, lunging at the air with drooling mouths and bared teeth. Julia reaches through the fence, pats them on their buffalo-sized heads, and kisses them through the chicken wire.

"Good, good doggies," says Julia, wiping rottweiler drool from her cheek.

"They're here for security," says Lina.

"They're here to rip my balls off," mutters my husband, who has recently taken to walking to the stable through 100 meters of swamp—rumored to have areas of quicksand—rather than pass by Honey and Bunny's security check.

In addition to Honey and Bunny, there's Moritz, a yapping rat dog. Moritz runs in little circles and yips and nips at our ankles. Julia and her friends adore Moritz. They carry him around like a baby. I try to pet him and he bites me. I'm sure Moritz has envisioned himself living in Aspen and being toted about town in a pink designer doggie carrier. Instead he's living in a barn with Honey, Bunny, fourteen horses, and dozens of mud-crusted adolescent girls. No bling in this place. No wonder he's pissed. A dozen cats, a gaggle of chickens, and two newly acquired dwarf roosters add to Moritz's torment. Julia enters a contest to name the roosters. Her choices are Elvis and Goliath. If she wins she gets ten fresh eggs.

Lina, a thirty-something single woman with dirty-blond hair and an extensive wardrobe of down vests with worn seams, lives with her family in a house attached to the stable. She runs the riding business. Her sister Lucy paints beautiful pictures of Lina's horses but never rides them, which makes me relate to her in an odd way. Lina's mother bakes cakes, takes care of the cat team, and goes for leashless walks with Honey and Bunny—a twice-daily event we try to avoid. Lina's father, as far as I can tell, spends most of his time speeding up and down the middle of the local highway in an electric wheelchair, on his way to the village shops to buy bakery goods, newspapers, and slabs of meat for Honey and Bunny. I'm not the only mother in town who has had to drive into a ditch to avoid a head-on collision with Herr Schwarz and his wheelchair.

"That guy should wear a helmet," says Julia.

☙

In addition to Julia's weekly riding lessons, she attends Lina's annual riding camp. We drop her off on a Monday morning and pick her up again on Friday. She comes home stuffed with cake and noodles and vegetarian schnitzel prepared by Lina's mother. She has dried gunk in her hair and tiny pieces of straw in her eyebrows.

"Why don't you ever take a shower while you're there?" I ask.

"I would," she says. "But I'm not too crazy about the *rat.*"

"The rat?"

"Lorenzo. He lives in the shower stall."

☙

I've been on lots of trail rides in my life, on slowpoke horses with names like Old Joe, Slumberboy, and Adagio. They went *hunka hunka hunka* in an easy tempo and carried me through various

American national parks on trails cushioned by pine needles. But as a child I had always wanted to really ride. I wanted to gallop on the beach with the wind in my hair and the world at my feet, and with a Carole King tune playing as the soundtrack to it all. But riding lessons in the USA were too pricey for my family. Instead I played the piano and conquered my twelve-year-old confusion by writing my own *Tapestry*-inspired songs about the boys inside my head, the ones with strong arms and gentle souls.

In the summer of 2008 we take Julia to De Panne, a Belgian town on the North Sea. We find a large stable offering beautiful horses suited for beach riding. Hesitant to send her by herself—and eager to fulfill my own teenage fantasies of riding next to the surf—I sign up to go along.

"Can Madame drive the horse?" asks the stable owner, a snippy Frenchwoman wearing jodhpurs.

"*Oui.*" I am sure the ride will be a comfortable sunset-inspired lumber through the dunes, with a stop for brie, wine, and a spectacular view.

"Are you crazy?" my husband whispers. "You haven't been on a horse since the sixth grade."

"I'll be fine," I say. "I used to go on rides like this in the States. These trail horses are trained to go slowly, especially with tourists on their backs."

"The horses here will be much faster," he says. "The tourists in Europe are thinner."

This turns out to be true. The riders are all between twelve and eighteen, sleek and outfitted, like Julia, in professional riding clothes. I am wearing jeans, tennis shoes, and a glossy silver bike helmet. The ultimate Ugly American, looking for a *Bonanza* adventure, European style.

"Can Madame really drive the horse?" the owner of the stable asks me, staring at my bike helmet.

"*Oui.*"

Julia puts the saddle on an Appaloosa named Rocket. I have to wait for her to help me because I have no idea how to saddle my horse, whose name is Thunder.

"Do not let the name scare you," the owner says. "Thunder, he is very old and very slow. He will be fine as long as you know how to drive him."

"Mom," Julia says. "You really don't have to go with me. I'll be fine."

"Julia, I need to go with you, at least the first time," I say. "Just to make sure you're okay. We are, after all, in a foreign country."

She stares at me with that look reserved by adolescent girls for their middle-aged mothers. Shifty-eyed, a little panicked, a little amused.

"What do you call this thing, anyway?" I ask.

"That's a stirrup, Mom. It's for your foot."

She hoists me onto Thunder's back. Thunder snorts and refuses to move, which I take as a good sign. "See?" I say to John, who's shaking his head and taking pictures. "He's old and slow, just like me."

John waits just a beat too long before he says, "You're not old, sweetie."

"*Merci.*" Julia leads me outside and ties Thunder to a post, an action that seems entirely unnecessary since he's not interested in going anywhere at all.

About ten other riders arrive in the ring. David, a guide who looks like he's auditioning for the equestrian version of *Baywatch*, enters on the back of a huge horse. Black Beauty has steaming nostrils and hooves the size of an average man's head. All at once I understand why this particular trail ride has attracted so many teenage girls. David smiles at us, his horse rears up and makes a horse noise that sounds like a broken scream, and the girls sigh in unison. Suntanned and brawny, David wears a tight-fitting T-shirt, riding pants, and those high leather boots that turn an already handsome guy into the stuff of dreams. He says hello to Julia and her cheeks turn pink. I am witnessing her first boy-induced blush.

"And you, Madame, you are the mother?"

"*Oui.*" I do not blush.

"Can you drive the horse, Madame?"

"*Oui.*"

"Let us go, then. *Allez!*"

Well.

The second those horses get into the dunes, they began to trot. Trot sounds like such a gentle word. Trotting is not gentle, especially if one has breasts. Thunder, whose specialty is following the other horses, trots along behind them. I can handle this on flat ground, but once we're in the hills I begin to sweat.

"Mommy, are you okay?" yells my daughter.

"*Oui*," I say. But not really.

"And now, we will make the GALLOP!" yells David from the front of the pack. It is at this point I notice he's carrying a whip.

The other riders, Julia included, take off. They look like part of an elegant equestrian ballet. I, on the other hand, find myself hanging off the side of the horse. My feet are out of the stirrups and I can't get them back in. My bike helmet has slipped over one eye.

One of the girls passes me, then another, until all of them are ahead of me. Not pleased to be trailing the others, Thunder picks up speed.

"Wait until we get to the open beach," I hear one of the girls yell. "Then we can really go fast!"

Jesus Christ. We are ten minutes into the two-hour ride, and I feel as if I've spent three days hanging off the side of the Eurostar.

"Help!" I yell. "Help!"

"*Arretez!!* Stop!" David shouts from the front.

"Mommy, are you okay?" Julia says.

I pull myself back onto the saddle, adjust my helmet and yank up my bra strap. Thunder eats dune grass.

"*Oui,*" I say, but I don't think she hears me.

"Your mother, she cannot drive the horse," says David to Julia.

"*Non,*" says Julia, with a newly acquired French accent. "But she is trying her best."

David talks into his cell phone. I understand only a few words of the tense conversation, but it's clear he's planning to throw me out of the group. Fine with me. It will take an hour, but I can walk back to the stable. Or limp. I feel as if my thighs have been beaten with a crowbar.

"Madame, you cannot drive," he says.

"*Oui.* I am so sorry. I thought this would be more like an American trail ride."

"But this is not America. Your bad driving is dangerous for all of us. You must go back."

"Okay," I say. "Will you take the horse?"

"*Non,* Madame, you must drive the horse back home. I will go with you. Clarise, one of our better drivers, she will take the group for the gallop on the waves."

I am now surrounded by a circle of glaring teenage girls, all of whom are ready to kill me for stealing David away from them.

"Julia, will you be okay?" I ask. She rolls her eyes, gathers the reins, and gallops away with the others. David, Black Beauty, Thunder, and I clump back toward the stable, but we ride on a path that leads us, for a short time, onto the beach. A strong ocean breeze stings my face, the surf crashes, and for a split second, with this muscled horse carrying me through the ocean's froth and this beautiful teenage boy-man giving me instructions, I remember what it's like to be twelve years old. From a distance I see the other girls, streaks of light racing against a dusky sky.

Wait for me, I want to shout. But they are too far away to hear.

Back in Germany, Julia continues her lessons at Lina's riding school. Watching Julia master these big animals takes my breath away. Her love for the sport comes from her love for animals—these particular animals. She talks to them in secret code and brings them carefully chosen snacks. She understands their needs and eccentricities. For instance, she knows Darty loves to bite the butt of any animal in front of him, and she knows that—due to an unfortunate experience with the Zirkus Trampolini offspring—he hates little kids. Over the years she has earned Darty's trust.

Music and riding, she loves both, even though they seem to be on opposite ends of the hobby scale. But it occurs to me that music's challenges are similar to those of riding. She climbs on a horse; she tackles a new piece of music. Both activities require patience and discipline; both tasks offer unique rewards but only after years of practice. When Carole King got rich and left the Brill Building for good, what did she do? She bought a ranch. There you go. Horses and music. Sometimes you can have both.

༄

Darty gets sick and needs an operation, which Lina can't afford. Julia canvasses the neighborhood carrying a coffee can decorated with photos and a sign that says SAVE DARTY. She hits up teachers for money and collects change from her classmates. She presents 120 euros to Lina, but it's not enough to pay for the surgery. I hear Lina is strapped for cash, so I hope she uses the money to buy horse chow. Darty goes on sabbatical. The girls don't ride him, but they groom him and feed him apples and take him for therapeutic walks around the pasture. Eventually, he recovers. He can't gallop, but Julia can ride him slowly around the ring. I cannot measure her joy.

We invest in a better helmet and a better pair of boots. We buy a protective vest for jumping and new pants in an adult size. I love to spy on her at the end of her lessons. I watch her slide from Darty's back and land with a splat in the muck. With her head thrown back she laughs at nothing at all, whispers in Darty's ear, and leads him into the stable for a drink of water. I don't know who's happier, the pony or the girl.

༄

Without warning Lina sells the horses and ponies. One day Julia goes for her lesson and they are gone, just like that. Rumors spread across the village. Lina's sick. She's pregnant. Legal problems.

"Financial difficulties," she tells the girls. Julia arrives home clutching a wad of money in her fist, money returned to us for lessons that have been canceled. She maintains her composure for about fifteen seconds, then begins to sob. She throws the cash on the floor.

"Gone. They are gone," she says. "I never even got to say goodbye."

"Oh, Julia," I say. "Lina loves those horses. I'm sure she sold them to a good person."

"What about Darty? Who will take care of Darty? Who will understand what he needs? He's very particular, you know."

"Maybe Lina made a list for the new owner." A list? My mother's instincts are failing me. "Maybe he'll live with a nice family with little kids."

"He hates little kids."

She cries about the pony. I cry because I recognize what has happened, why her heart is broken. She thought she was in control, but she wasn't. My words to her sound hollow, but I do that mother thing, not exactly lying, but skirting around the truth, trying to find a comforting sentence. I'm angry with Lina, sickened by the thought of poor Darty ending up in a German glue factory, and wondering if anything in my parent's bag of tricks will help. I babble on and on about new chapters in life, moving forward, any cliché I can find. I tell her that all of her hours of grooming and braiding and shoveling manure, all of the time she put into understanding Darty's oddities, all of the whispering and coaxing meant something to Darty, for sure.

"Not enough," she says. "He left."

"He didn't leave you, Jul. He was sent away."

"How is that different?" She eats her dinner in silence, her eyes dull and sad. She doesn't touch the piano or smile for days. Darty is gone. He got her from girlhood to adulthood, then, against his will, dumped her there with no way to get back.

Lina needed money. She sold Darty. It's that simple, but so complicated to the mind of a trusting twelve-year-old, a kid who thought all she needed to do to keep a friend forever was care. Sometimes love just isn't enough. I knew she'd find out sooner or later.

∾

Two months later I find Darty. His new owner operates a riding school several towns away from us. I'm so relieved Darty is alive and healthy that I agree to let Julia ride there. She cannot sleep the night before the first session, but I can't tell whether it's worry or excitement that's keeping her awake.

I take a photo of the two of them when they're reunited: Girl and pony, tangled together in a blur of hair and mane. She rides Darty around the huge indoor hall, and the teacher says to me: "Those two are made for each other, at least for now. Before long she'll switch to one of the bigger horses."

"But we're here for Darty," I say. "She loves Darty."

"That will change," he says.

Julia rides Darty to the far end of the ring and then heads back in our direction, happy and cautious all at once.

Once again I'm reminded of what it's like to be twelve years old. Insight, it turns out, is the beginning of adulthood. I sit on an old wooden bench and watch Julia glide around the arena. She signals every time she passes me, just like a toddler waving at her mother from a wooden carousel horse, raising her hand to greet me, until, finally, the ride is over.

Little Big Soul

I finish my second set of piano music with "Music of Goodbye." It's in D minor, but I end the piece in F major so it doesn't sound so dark. I have to be careful of that; since leaving New York City I have been drawn to sad songs.

I lower the fallboard on the Yamaha grand and join my friends Katja and Conny in the empty cocktail bar on one side of the castle lobby. The other guests sit outside on the terrace. It's a beautiful evening at Schlosshotel Lerbach. Almost no one stays inside on a night like this.

"I love that song," says Conny. "But it's so sad."

"Yeah, well, sad is good," I say.

We drink wine, laugh about our children, and sift through our stories. We might be any three women enjoying an evening away from the family-career balancing act, except for one thing. Conny is dying. We know it; she knows it. We wiggle around the subject.

"What's the one thing in life you'd most like to do?" asks Katja.

"I'm doing it," I say. "I'm writing a book about playing the piano. And you?"

"Just once, I'd love to swim with dolphins," says Katja. This is typical Katja. She shuns makeup, she bakes bread, she wears organic cotton in earthy tones, and she wants to swim with dolphins. She probably already speaks their language.

We look at Conny. "Your turn," I say.

"I don't know," she says. "I just don't know." Bad topic. Conny is on the waiting list for a bone-marrow transplant. For her, getting through the day is enough. I sip my drink.

I wish we could continue the conversation outside, but the evening air is too brisk for Conny, who must avoid catching a cold. She says she's in training, like a high-powered athlete.

"Wait!" she says, "I know what I'd like to do. I'd like to walk, very slowly, to the top of a big mountain on a clear day, just so I could look down at the distance I had covered and shout, 'I did it! I made it to the top!'"

This is the stuff of anthems and hymns. Move on, stay strong, follow your dreams, and never give up. In worn-out song lyrics and overplayed movie themes, all of us become capable of forging streams, climbing hills, and crossing oceans. But for Conny, the idea of a mountaintop goes beyond the cliché. If she wants to get to her particular summit she's going to need one hell of a pair of hiking boots, a chemo-proof navigation system, and safety cables of braided steel.

The lights flicker in the dusk. The trees stand guard in the castle park. I wait for the bartender to light the lone candle sitting on our table.

᠗

Two people die in this story: a mother and her teenage daughter. There's some music, too, but not nearly enough to make a difference. I tried to escape from Conny and her family a couple of times. I wanted to run to a fantasyland where fucked-up things don't happen to good people, especially good people who happen to be my friends. But I never got very far. My feet moved, but my heart was stuck. I was screwed. Or blessed. Or maybe a little of both. You can't write a song about this. Trust me, I've tried.

∽

"Mommy," says my three-year-old daughter, Julia, "Look. Look here." Julia stands next to an easel in the kindergarten playroom. She is spattered with bright blue paint, just like the little girl next to her.

"Wow," I say. "That's a very, uh, blue painting."

"Not the painting, Mom. Look. My friend. I have a friend."

"Oh!" I say. "Hello."

"HELLO!"

The tiny girl is wearing a baseball cap, and her balance is shaky. She has circles of paint on her face.

"What's your name?" I ask.

"LISA!!!"

"Lisa is my friend," says Julia.

"MY FRIEND!" says Lisa. "WE ARE BLUE!"

"I am Robin," I say. "I am not blue."

"ROBIN! ROBIN! YOU ARE MY FRIEND!"

"Thank you," I say.

"I AM LISA!"

"Lisa is my friend," says Julia.

∽

When I first meet Conny Traupe, Lisa's mom, she's wearing a squirrel costume. I am dressed as a mouse. We are rehearsing for the annual Christmas play at the Wahlscheid Montessori Kindergarten, where Julia and Lisa are enrolled. Every Christmas the parents present a play for the children. No pressure on the kids to perform, but plenty of pressure on the adults to come up with meaningful holiday entertainment for thirty preschoolers. Rehearsals are fun. We sing *Stille Nacht*, choreograph our rodent ballet, and laugh ourselves silly.

The kindergarten mainstreams disabled children with "regular" kids, a distinction that grows fuzzier for me with each day. A kid is a kid. Turns out this is true even when the kid—Lisa—has had two major operations for brain cancer, several brutal rounds of experimental chemotherapy, and enough radiation to light up half of the European night.

Conny, who is my age, works as an elementary-school teacher. She has taken time off to care for Lisa during the extensive therapy she needs to get her back on her feet. Because of the complications of the second surgery, Lisa has had to relearn basic skills like walking, talking, even eating.

Conny's optimism scares me, but I also understand it. "I keep going, no matter what," she says. "And I stay positive, because, really, it's the only sensible choice. What am I going to do? Kill myself, go bonkers, or deal. I deal."

A parent is a parent.

❦

One night, crouched in the wings of our makeshift backstage area in the school gymnasium, Conny begins telling me the details of Lisa's condition. She was born with Rubinstein-Taybi syndrome, which means she's small in stature—teeny-tiny, in fact—and mentally disabled. Some children with this condition—like Lisa—have an increased risk of developing cancerous tumors, including certain kinds of brain tumors.

Lisa doesn't say much, but she shouts out each sentence as if she's broadcasting the world's best news. She sings, she laughs, she sings some more; hearing her voice in the kindergarten corridor is like tumbling into an unexpected puddle of sunshine. Conny takes Lisa to music class, to horseback riding lessons (to improve her balance), to art classes, to speech therapists, to doctors and researchers and nutritionists. She also takes her out for ice cream, to art museums, to children's theater productions, to the zoo. She is the best mother I know.

Twice a year doctors run a battery of tests on Lisa to determine whether new brain tumors are developing. I wonder how Conny stands waiting for the results.

"I deal," she reminds me.

One night at rehearsal for the Christmas play, I lean on a ladder backstage and listen to Lisa's latest medical report: "The doctors say that Lisa's brain cancer has a strong chance of recurring. But she is one of the first kids to have undergone this new chemo. So, of course, she has a good chance." Conny is sporting a mud-colored furry hat with squirrel ears. I adjust my mouse whiskers and turn away from her. Her optimism overwhelms me.

෧෨

Lisa graduates from three years of kindergarten, stays healthy, and begins attending a special school for disabled kids.

Then Conny gets sick. I hear this through the kindergarten grapevine. Stage Two breast cancer. How can this happen? It happens. But still, okay, Stage Two is not as bad as it could be. She opts for a lumpectomy, radiation, and chemo. The chemotherapy almost kills her and is discontinued after a few weeks. She spends the next year trying to recover, not from the surgery or the cancer, but from the catastrophic effects of the chemo.

I hear all of this thirdhand, because I don't call her. I don't want to intrude on her privacy, I tell myself. But really, I don't want the unfairness of her situation to shatter my notion of *the way things should be.* With some relief I hear a rumor that Conny doesn't want visitors—that she wants to be left alone. Good. I'm off the hook. I resort to dropping baskets of organic stuff on her doorstep. I leave without ringing the bell and tiptoe away as quickly as I can. I'm afraid to get too close. Cancer isn't contagious. But friendship is. I imagine her watching me from her bedroom window as I scurry back to my easy-breezy perfect little life. I can almost hear her voice calling me as I follow the winding road that leads back to my village.

Oh no you don't, Ms. Goldsby. Not so fast. You come back here and deal with me.

But I don't go back. I keep driving, ashamed of my reluctance to get involved, to get too close. Later I will realize that Conny Traupe had set her sights on me for a reason. She was first and foremost a mother to Lisa. But she was also a teacher, and I had a lot to learn.

⁊⁞

"I'm feeling much better now," Conny says to me on the phone, six months after my last basket drop. "I want you to come and have coffee with me."

That I can do.

I arrive at her house on a crisp November day. Lisa greets me with a demonstration of how she has learned to cut paper with blunt scissors. I haven't seen Lisa for months. She's still small but has gained weight. She's dressed in a dark green sweater and pants, with a coordinated baseball cap that covers her bald head.

"ROBIN!"

"Lisa!"

"WHERE'S JULIA?"

"At school."

"SHE'S MY FRIEND!"

Lisa joins us for a piece of cake at the dining table and then begins playing with a pink balloon, batting it around the living room. She is a tiny ballerina, dancing to music I can't hear.

"I need you to help me," Conny says.

"Uh—sure," I say. "Anything at all." Maybe she'll request a ride to a doctor's appointment or help with an English translation.

"You walk for exercise, right?"

"Uh, actually I run. Or maybe 'jog slowly' would be a better description."

"Can you speed-walk instead?"

"Guess so. Never tried it. Why?"

"I want you to walk with me. Three times a week. And I want you to talk to me, about things that have nothing to do with illness. I'm sick of being sick. I want you to talk about yourself, about your music, about your kids. I need the distraction. My life has turned into one big medical discussion, and if I'm going to recover I need to get away from that."

"I—"

"Think about it. Maybe I'm too slow for you, as far as the exercise goes. But maybe we can try. Just once."

Try. That I can do.

❧

She is not too slow for me. We walk three times a week. We walk through hellish rain and toe-curling heat and pinprick ice storms. We make fun of the chubby Nordic Walkers. We talk about men and romance. We discuss art and theater and the latest books we've read. Sometimes she speaks English and I respond in German. Sometimes it's the other way around. We walk and talk our way through two years of our lives.

We discuss George Bush and the botched election that led to his disastrous presidency.

We talk about World War II, the Holocaust, and the guilt passed on from one generation of Germans to the next.

We trade recipes for vegetable lasagna and apple cake.

We argue about separation of church and state.

We talk a lot about our kids. Conny tells me about Lisa's latest triumph at school, the way she laughs when she goes riding, how she adores her music-therapy class. She talks about Lisa's most recent challenge; I talk about what my kids are facing. I feel guilty when I describe my son's aversion to math or my daughter's inability to do her homework without talking to an imaginary man who lives on her eraser. I whine about these things and wonder how she puts up with me. But she does. She listens and nods and gives advice. A challenge is a challenge. A kid is a kid. A friend is a friend.

Conny gets inside my head, tapping into the place that most artists guard. Walking with her becomes a sort of jailbreak for my pent-up fantasy world. I talk to her about story ideas and music projects, and find myself slipping into stream-of-consciousness monologues that exhilarate me.

I play background piano music to make a living, but I have a deep fear of playing concerts or recitals for people who might actually listen. Give me a room with fifty people drinking and chatting with each other and I have no problem playing. Put those same fifty people in a recital hall and ask me to perform for them and I fall apart.

"I don't get it," Conny says. "You've got these nice CDs, so why don't you do an actual concert program? You have to get out of the cocktail lounge and begin playing for real audiences. I'll come and sit in the front row."

"No." I am firm about this. "I can't play a formal concert in front of an audience. The idea terrifies me—Voice of Doom would have a field day. I have anxiety attacks, Conny, and they paralyze me. Just thinking about playing in a concert hall makes me sick. Can't do it. No way. Never."

"Get over it," she says. "Get over yourself. *Augen zu und durch.*" Close your eyes and move forward. She is an expert at this.

∾

I get to know Conny's husband, Eddy. He's a quiet guy with a bushy mustache and a gentle sense of humor. I think maybe he is made of iron, or diamond dust, or some yet-to-be-discovered hard-as-rock composite. He takes care of Lisa and Conny and still keeps his balance. Maybe he is made of love.

My family is invited to Conny's house for a Sunday afternoon cake-and-music party. John brings his upright bass.

"CURTIS! JOHN! ROBIN! JULIA!" Lisa shouts when we arrive. "BASS!" She has summed up the essence of my family in five words.

Conny pulls an African drum out of a closet, Eddy places a toy xylophone on the table, and we set up an electric keyboard next to the window. Julia sings; I play; Curtis whacks the drum. And Lisa dances around John and his bass in a joyful trance. At least a dozen times we play and sing a politically incorrect song about three Chinese guys and a contrabass. Every time the song ends, Lisa throws her arms up in the air.

"MORE! MORE JOHN! MORE BASS!"

More everything, I think. More time, is what I mean.

∽

Two years after our first walk together, Conny begins to cancel our sessions—under the weather, tired, sore throat. I try not to worry, but I do.

She's diagnosed with acute leukemia, resulting from the damage done to her bone marrow by the chemo she had undergone after the breast-cancer surgery. Conny opts for a bone-marrow transplant and puts herself on a list for a donor. She agrees to be the poster child for a donor drive in our community, and her picture is plastered on telephone poles and storefront windows all over our neighborhood. She knows the odds of finding a donor for herself are small. But she hopes that someone else on the transplant list might be helped.

I volunteer to assist with the event, and the Bone Marrow Drive Committee turns me down, not because they don't want me, but because they already have too many helpers. Community leaders, teachers, and neighbors take over like a Birkenstock-clad army carrying heaping plates of cakes and cookies as weapons. Sell a cupcake, save a life. I contribute a box of CDs to raise money, and Schlosshotel Lerbach donates a gourmet lunch for two to the auction.

I'm stunned by the positive energy. It becomes a festival of sorts, a celebration of community goodwill, and it's easy to forget that the whole thing started with one woman's tragedy. Over 1,000 potential donors show up and agree to be tested. Conny's smiling face adorns the cloth banners welcoming visitors to the event. Conny herself sits at home with Lisa and tries to find the energy to fold her daughter's clean laundry.

A few days after the donor drive, Conny learns that she's an adult-onset victim of a rare congenital disease called Fanconi anemia. Because of this, doctors tell her she will not survive a bone-marrow transplant. She visits a specialist in Switzerland who advises her to accept her fate and die comfortably. She refuses. She might be able to give up on herself, but she wants to stick around for Lisa.

Conny receives a blood transfusion and feels more energetic. We discuss her situation over dinner one night in a casual outdoor restaurant in nearby Siegburg. The balmy weather, the scent of rosemary and lavender, a perfect glass of chilled Riesling—all of these things make our conversation easy and cheerful.

"This sounds weird," she says, "but I'm comforted by this news. At least now I know why I'm sick. Not knowing why was driving me nuts."

She's not strong enough, so we've stopped walking. We've stopped moving. We're sitting still and the world is spinning forward, faster and faster, smudging the crooked lines that connect denial to truth. She will die soon, and she won't allow me, not for one second, to believe it. I offer my half-empty glass in a toast to my friend, she offers her half-full glass in return, and we drink to her determination.

I drop her off at home. Lisa greets us at the door wearing light-yellow pajamas with feet in them, clutching a cloth baby doll in one arm, a stuffed bunny in the other.

"ROBIN!" She yells, with sleepy eyes and a lopsided grin. "WHERE'S JOHN? WHERE'S THE BASS?"

"Not here," I say. "John has a concert. This was a night for your mama and me." I hug Lisa and jump back in the car. Conny has left her beige cotton jacket on the backseat.

"Your jacket!" I shout out the window.

"Keep it," she says. "I'll get it next time."

Next time.

I drive away and arrive at my own front door. I hang Conny's jacket on my coatrack, next to my daughter's raincoat.

᠙᠍᠊ᠣ

While I'm on holiday with my family in the Austrian Alps, a transplant match is found for Conny. She insists on going through with the procedure. I'm on a mountain, she is starting to climb one. She has convinced herself and her doctors that maybe, just maybe, she'll survive. Accompanied by Eddy, she leaves for the clinic in Düsseldorf, armed with books on spirituality, meditation, and nutritional advice for bone-marrow recipients. And music. She takes her music with her, too.

Lisa is heartbroken when Conny leaves home but finds comfort in the arms of Doro, a day-care provider who has watched over her for years. Doro is strong and beautiful, with soft arms and softer eyes. Her family loves Lisa. Conny has chosen well.

The first few weeks are filled with tests and intense chemo treatments to prepare Conny for the transplant. Eddy and Doro keep me informed. Eddy is noncommittal about Conny's condition. Doro tells me things I don't want to hear. Conny has good days and bad. She doesn't want visitors. But Eddy calls me one afternoon and says she wants to talk to me. Her voice is shiny and confident and she's sure the procedure will go smoothly, that she is just a few months away from having a normal life. She is the Conny I've always known: the walker, the mother, the woman who believes she can do anything if she stays positive and keeps moving forward. The transplant is scheduled for eleven the next morning.

"Here's what I want you to do," she says. "This sounds crazy, but I want you to play the piano for me as the transplant is taking place. I'll be hooked up to an IV in my room. I want you to play to make those new cells feel welcome, sort of a cocktail party for the new bone marrow."

We laugh, but I know she is halfway serious. Every part of me trusts this will work. Eddy calls me the next morning at eleven. I carry the phone to the piano and place the receiver next to me. I open the doors onto the balcony and visualize the music floating over the valley and wafting toward her hospital room in Düsseldorf. I play the concert of my life. For over an hour I play—for Conny, for Lisa, for Eddy, for myself.

Stillness settles around me. The foamy lace curtains by the piano move in a gentle breeze. I stop playing, pick up the phone, and say, "Hello?"

But no one is there. Just air and silence, hope and sadness. I don't know if she has heard anything at all. But I do know that for the last hour, I've been playing music that counts, if not for her, then for me.

A month later she dies. Eddy asks me to play for her funeral. Conny had left a list of guests to be invited, a list of her favorite flowers, and instructions for me to play her favorite songs.

I can't imagine being able to overcome my grief. I can't imagine overcoming my fear of playing for a listening audience.

"Get over yourself," I hear her say. "*Augen zu und durch.*"

I call my concert-pianist friend Robin Spielberg in New York to ask her how the hell I'm supposed to cope with my raging emotions and still be able to perform. "The piano will rescue you every time," she says. "Just play for your friend. The rest will fall into place."

This I can do.

Hundreds of people show up for Conny's service, many of them her former students. Lisa's classmates come in wheelchairs, pushed by parents and teachers. I play songs I have written. I hear Lisa when she enters the church with Eddy and Doro.

"HELLO!!! HELLO!!!"

I look over my shoulder and see her shaking hands with people on the aisle, thanking them for coming. Conny would be so proud of her. Lisa is smiling and golden and, yes, like sunshine.

The minister Conny had selected, a lovely man named Theo, conducts the service, which is dignified, meaningful, and personal. He introduces me and I play a piece I have written for Conny, a song called "Mountaintop." Maybe she hears it, but probably not. I finish the piece and slide into the pew next to my husband and children.

Lisa turns around, looks me right in the eye and shouts, "ARE YOU TAKING A BREAK ALREADY?"

Even though we're crying, we laugh out loud. It is a blurt of joy, and it is the best music I can imagine.

Theo speaks some more, I play, we sing, we light candles. Lisa accompanies her mother's casket to the cemetery. Eddy buries his beautiful wife.

Later, I will think back on the many conversations Conny and I had on our walks—about my reluctance to play in front of a listening audience, about my paralyzing anxiety attacks, about facing a challenge head-on. She is gone, and she is still speaking to me, still teaching, still preventing me from running away from what's most important. Every time I play a concert I will hear her voice, and it comes from—where? Maybe from heaven, maybe from the piano, maybe from nowhere at all.

∾

Two years after her mother's death, Lisa's brain cancer returns. Right before the end I am given the honor of visiting her at home. I don't see a dying child; I see a tiny, translucent angel-like version of Conny, a fifteen-year-old girl who has completed her life's work and is ready to move on. She is peaceful and quiet and content, her little big soul hovering between now and next. Eddy never leaves her side.

I play for Lisa's memorial service, sitting at the same piano in the same church, looking out at the same faces I had seen at Conny's funeral. We are not wiser, but we are older. We do not have Lisa's sunny personality to help us through this funeral. God, we need her today.

I have chosen a Sarah McLaughlin piece called "Angel" to play for the recessional. As the first chords unfold, Eddy walks down the aisle of the church, followed by Lisa's tiny casket carried by men I don't know. Three hundred people rise to their feet in a silent tribute to Lisa's life. I continue to play and watch the congregation—including my husband and children—follow Eddy out of the church and to the cemetery, where Lisa will be buried next to her mother. From the day I met Conny and Lisa, I had known I would end up right here, in this spot, playing one last song for the two of them. I play until the last people have gone, put my head against the piano, and cry as hard as I've ever cried.

I feel a hand on my shoulder. I look up and see Katja, who has waited for me. We walk together to Lisa's and Conny's graves, strain to hear the minister's words, watch the casket as it is lowered into the ground, and stand in line to toss a shovelful of earth and a rose into the empty space before us.

"ROBIN! YOU ARE MY FRIEND!" I miss Lisa's bell-like voice almost as much as I miss her mother's friendship.

⌐∽

Years later I think back on that night in the cocktail lounge with Katja and Conny. I don't remember much about the funerals, but that tipsy conversation with my friends about lifelong wishes and dolphins and mountaintops? It rushes back to me all the time, popping into my mind in perfect detail, like a favorite childhood song.

Conny sits in a front-row seat—as she promised—paying attention to just about everything I do. Her presence in my life inspired countless stories, an entire CD of compositions, a novel. She made me a better mother, a better musician, a better friend. It feels cheap to write about her courage—nothing I could say would do her justice—but I'm sure of one thing: Conny Traupe would want the world to know that she and her daughter changed me, for the better.

I deal.

Maybe in Conny's last drug-induced dream she made it to her imagined mountaintop. Maybe instead of taking the tedious and rocky path back to the bottom, she chose to offer her arms to the clouds, her spirit to the wind, and her courage to those of us who still miss her wisdom.

&

Come down you angel,
Come down and sing,
Bring me a piece of sky.

Scatter your stardust,
Like snow in the trees,
Bring me a piece of sky.

The Glass Piano

The dimples in a child's closed fist inspire a lullaby; the devil's swish of falling leaves on a gusty November morning prompts a wistful melody in a minor key; trumpets herald an athlete's record-setting victory; the ancient truths of romantic love cue the violins. A fear of death brings on diminished chords played by an organ; the reality of death calls for an angel's harp. We save the bass for walking, and the flutes for new life, new hope, and whimsical stories about eager children with brightly colored buckets of mud and sand. When we laugh we hear a pennywhistle, the trill of a clarinet, a trombone sliding into a note that's not quite what we hoped for. Sorrow is outlined by a bow sweeping across a cello's strings, or maybe an oboe's reedy whine or the muted sound of a bugle played by a soldier with a raised head and a heavy heart.

Life has little to do with music. But music has everything to do with life.

I play the piano. And the way I play—in turns halting, flowing, silly, or sad—reflects the way I live: On-off, high-low, fluffed up, trampled down, needed or needy, ignored by many, loved by a few.

Sometimes I imagine the piano is made of glass, a sculpture with rounded edges and sharp corners that are fragile and cracked in vulnerable spots and bulletproof in others, protecting and exposing me all at once. Before I start to play this evening, I gaze over the lowered lid of my crystal piano. I imagine a chiffon sky embroidered with threads of black silk, and a smudged horizon framing an ocean's twilight-hued tapestry.

Look up. There. Breaking away from the crowded night, a runaway star, or maybe a forgotten song, slices through a cloudless sky and plops into the swollen sea. The star pierces my memory and plunges into the liquid past, taking me along for the ride. I'm part of an underwater fantasy ballet, and the moonlight paints an iridescent backdrop for the random pictures dancing around me. Silent slow-motion shadows move at the same tempo as my heartbeat, and a hesitant melody unwinds in my head—one note at a time—like the worn-out song inside a little girl's jewelry box. Mine was pink, with an inch-high yellow-haired plastic ballerina who turned on her toes whenever the music began to play. I can still hear the notes, but I forget the song.

Flashes of my childhood swim past me in a warped music video without an audio track. My father plays a soundless snare drum, my mother mouths the words to a snappy tune. My brother and sister, with sleepy eyes and devious smiles, laugh and poke their fingers in my ribs. One robust grandmother conducts an aging choir from a church pulpit, while the other grandmother—bejeweled, bewigged, and befrocked in bright red Ultrasuede—sits at an enormous green upright piano. Her back is straight; her foot beats the plush wall-to-wall carpet in perfect time.

For a split second I feel my parents lifting me toward a fuzzy light, grasping my hands and pushing me away, all at once. In the time it takes to mentally recite the words to "Bye Bye Blackbird," "Build Me Up Buttercup," and a handful of Blood Sweat and Tears tunes, I grow up. I travel from overalls to bikini to prom dress while Carole King sings lyrics I can't yet understand and a boy named Mark steals my heart by promising me a life I can't imagine. We carve our names in a bench overlooking the city of Pittsburgh and watch two rivers ending and a third river beginning—a water dance that needs a song, which I won't write for another forty years.

I leave one home and find another, and another, crisscrossing city streets and state lines and oceans until all the homes I've ever had morph into a marine subdivision of look-alike undersea castles. My friends—choreographed like a team of synchronized swimmers wearing sequined bathing caps and matching tank suits—wave goodbye and wave hello and wave goodbye again. I watch them drift away while tears gather behind my eyes in the exact spot where songs are born.

I feel the strong arms of the man I married, coaxing me into a velvet-lined pocket of warm water. It is here, as he spins by my side, my untamed ribbons of hair tangled in his graceful fingers, that I remember the miracle of love. Two babies—a girl and boy—swim in tiny circles at my feet, the circles widening to vast loops as our children grow up in double-time, triple-time, thrashing through the water, going as fast as they can until they dissolve into tiny points of light—underwater stars that shoot to the surface, shatter the water's edge, and catapult into the future, where they belong. I call after them, but they're already gone.

People move on. A song remains.

From my seat at the glass piano, I see a silver path of starlight—a trail of sparkling breadcrumbs tossed on a scrap of charcoal-hued linen. The sky promises, of course it does, to lead me back home. But the piano promises more: a nocturne, a jazz waltz, a hoedown, a romp. It offers bebop or hip-hop, techno or no-go, a prelude, an etude, or maybe just an easy melody to document a not-so-complicated life. That's enough.

The bench I sit on is solid and secure. I'm not lost in the stars, but maybe they are lost in me—unfinished pieces drowning in possibility, undiscovered songs waiting to be claimed. There's not enough time to play through all of them. So I must choose. Do I practice something new, or stick to melodies that remind me of who I used to be?

"Play something you know," my father often says to me. And then we laugh. Because we both know how much I have to learn. Still.

This piano isn't made of glass, or mirrors, or smoky illusions. Smudged with the fingerprints of other musicians, the ebony surface reflects what's left of the evening. The perfect rows of hammers, pins, felts, and strings startle me with their diminutive beauty. The silence tempts me.

I touch the keys, face the night, and remember what I know. A place. Or a time. Or maybe even you.

That's when the music begins.

PART TWO: SECOND ENDING

The Apricot Tree

Go right at the rotary and take the third exit, says Kate, the uppity British voice of our navigation system.

"What rotary? Where?"

"Like you can even call this a rotary," says John. We're in Villefranche sur Saône, France, a bit north of Lyon, searching for the home of Jean Auray, the award-winning luthier who has agreed to build John's new double bass. Any good musician will tell you that a quality instrument is the extension of an artist's soul, and John is looking to expand his soulfulness. Throughout his career he has dreamed of finding a bass that's comfortable to play, with a warm, clear, punchy sound and consistent tone across its entire range.

Monsieur Auray's home and workshop must be around here somewhere; Kate just needs to find it. We're packed into our mid-sized car with two very tall teenage kids and the bass John currently plays, a factory-made German instrument built after World War II. Building the new bass will take the better part of a year and several meetings requiring trips from Cologne to Lyon, a drive that typically takes six hours. Today, with the French *autoroute* traffic, a break for lunch at a French Ikea, and numerous rest stops, it has taken us a bit longer. We're a little cranky.

"Just about there!" I shout toward the back seats. Silence. With John's German bass packed between the two kids, I cannot see them. For all I know Curtis and Julia jumped out of the car somewhere around Nancy.

"Mom, I'm thirsty," says a muffled voice.

"Me too."

"Just a few more minutes," I say.

"They've got some nerve calling this a traffic circle," says John. "It's more like a triangle. Wait, that's the third exit!"

"No it's not, it's the fourth. There wasn't a third."

"How can there be a fourth if there wasn't a third?"

Take the third exit, says Kate. She is agitated by the French traffic regulations, or lack of them.

We drive around in a triangle-circle for a few minutes while we huff and mutter and blame each other for being lost.

Take the third exit, says Kate.

"Perhaps this is the French idea of a circle."

"Maybe it was the best they could do at the time. You know, ancient city and all that."

"*Non*," says my husband, who is now speaking in a French accent, quite a party trick for a boy from Kentucky. "They were sick of the circle. They had a better idea. It is like a circle, only not a circle. It is a circle with corners."

"Isn't that called an intersection?" says Curtis from the back seat.

Please take the third exit, says Kate, using the tone of voice she assumes right before she resorts to the silent treatment.

"There, that's it!" I yell.

"That's a brick wall," says John.

"Okay! Then take this one! Here!"

"This is not an exit, this is a driveway. It's very French. The highway looks like the driveway, and the driveway looks like—"

"Look out!" I yell as we swerve to avoid hitting a lorry that's entering the triangle.

"Don't overreact! Everything is fine. Stay calm." Bass players are known for statements like this.

The French word for car crash is *carambolage*; it's one of my favorite words, but I'd prefer not to use it today. Out of options, we exit the rotary on the same road we used to enter it, drive two blocks, perform the *demi-tour*—the French version of the U-turn— and miraculously find ourselves at 888 route de Riottier, the exact address of Monsieur Auray's workshop.

You have reached your destination, says Kate. *Bonne journée.*

"*Mon Dieu!*" says John.

"Are you sure this is it?" I ask. I climb out of the car and brush baguette crumbs from my jacket. I had envisioned something quainter, perhaps a small chateau with hand-carved dwarves lining a cobblestone walkway leading to an antique oak door. But this place looks like the stark entrance to a French fort. No dwarves here. Later I will discover that many homes in Lyon are bleak on the outside but glorious once you get inside—it's a style that goes back hundreds of years.

The back doors to the car open, and the kids tumble out and unfold themselves into upright positions. They remind me of pop-up tents. I do believe they've grown since the last rest stop.

"Isn't this exciting?" I say.

"It looks like a jail," says Curtis. "Do you think they have drinks at this place?"

"Look," says Julia. "Pigeons!"

We park in front of a tiny plaque with Monsieur's name and logo on it, and ring the bell.

We wait. John rings again. We can't hear the bell ringing, so we're not sure if it's working. We wait some more.

"It is like a doorbell, only not a doorbell," says John. He's wound up, and I can understand why. He's about to meet the man who will devote the next six months of his life to creating the bass of his dreams. I'm not so excited, mainly because we have just driven 800 kilometers and we're standing in an alleyway in front of a cement shack. Maybe this is an elaborate French ruse.

John first met Jean Auray in 2008, at a bass convention in Paris. He played several of Jean's instruments, one after another, and realized he had found a great luthier—an artisan who matched and even surpassed the work of many legendary bass makers. John's search for an older instrument that would fit his needs was replaced with the thrill of having a new bass built to his specifications.

Monsieur Auray finally opens the door to his workshop and shouts out—in broken English—a few hearty words of welcome. We respond in broken French. We make introductions. He invites us inside. The chill of winter slips away as we walk into a carpenter's golden oasis of wood and warmth. What a difference from the outside of the building. We climb a long curvy staircase, and it occurs to me that every bass-related business we've visited is up a flight or two of stairs. The place smells a little like a forest and a lot like varnish. A fine coating of sawdust covers every surface, and I'm reminded this isn't a showroom, but a workshop. A heap of curlicue wood shavings is piled under the table, as if someone scalped Pinocchio and left the trimmings on the floor.

Madame Auray, a beautiful Englishwoman who was raised in Paris, greets us and serves coffee and biscuits. Her first name is Juliet. She is rail-thin and moves through the workshop like a nimble-footed cat. She picks up odd scraps of paper and used coffee cups while she talks to me and chats with the kids in both English and French. Curtis and Julia are learning French at school, but they're shy about using it. I spent years speaking French in Haiti, but I sound like a cavewoman. Juliet glides back and forth between the two languages, making tiny corrections, introducing new words to us, and making sure John and Jean understand each other. In just sixty minutes of observing her, I know she's the quintessential multitasking artist's wife—interpreter, soother of the bruised ego, mother, mind reader, and bottle washer. I suspect she's also the family accountant.

A wooden lion's head with a menacing face—the topmost ornament of a bass that Auray is building for another musician— stands guard over the room. While John talks to Jean, I wander around the workshop with Juliet and peek into its attached rooms. Auray builds his own instruments, but he also repairs and sells other basses. The workshop has several smaller rooms attached to the main space, each one holding basses waiting to be repaired, basses that have been rescued from abusive homes, and a few basses that will never be played again but hold sentimental value. Even the basses with cracked bodies, rutted fingerboards, split seams, and broken tailpieces seem dignified. I hear the passion in Jean's voice as he describes his craft. Even though I don't understand much of his French, I know he agrees with me. The bass—strong and feminine and such an intimate part of my husband's life—might be the most physically beautiful of all musical instruments.

John has chosen the Auray bass for its lush sound—clear and round and bottom-rich, perfect for a jazz musician. In addition, the Auray is compact and transportable, with a nontraditional removable neck. The flight case for the Auray bass, called the *Nanoo*, is still oversized according to airline regulations, but most carriers will take it. They won't be happy about it, but they'll take it.

"Never say you are traveling with the *bass*," says Jean. "Say it is the *cello-bass*."

"Cello-bass?" It is like a cello, but not a cello. I wonder what the baggage handlers will have to say about this.

"I will *modify* your bass with the removable neck, but first I must *obtain* the concept of your sound." Jean's favorite English words are *modify* and *obtain*; they are fancy words for his limited vocabulary, and he uses them with gusto. Fine-boned and handsome, Jean has thick dark hair, fluttering hands, and intense blue eyes, the kind of eyes that take in too much at once and make snap judgments—usually correct—about people and art and music. I get the feeling we're being scoped out, interviewed and evaluated as potential adoptive parents for one of his bass children, and that one false move, one ugly American moment, and we'll be back on the *autoroute*, squashed in the car with the collapsible kids, arguing with Kate, *modifying* our plans, and trying to *obtain* another luthier.

"Now we must obtain the measurements," he says.

Curtis, Julia, and I sit in the corner with Juliet, eating our cookies and looking at pictures of other Auray basses.

John unpacks his older bass. Though it's a nonpedigreed instrument, it has a nice voice that records well. It's important for him to have a second bass that feels like this one, but with a more consistent tone.

"This is the sound I like," John says, as he plays several passages. Jean cocks his head to one side, leans into the music, and smiles.

"*Oui*," he says. "It sounds very beautiful. Only the new bass, the modified bass, perhaps she will be just as good. Perhaps she will be better."

"*Oui, oui*," says John. "I hope so."

"This I think is not a problem," says Jean. Both men are smiling. The challenge has been accepted, and if all goes well, both of them will win.

I walk over to Jean's worktable and look through a large window. The soft browns and grays of the Lyon winter make a perfect backdrop for the aged tree in the center of the garden, whose twisted trunk and gnarled limbs stretch toward the corners of the stone terrace. There's a song about this tree, and if I stand here long enough, I'm sure I'll hear it.

"Oh," says Monsieur. "You see the apricot tree!"

"It's amazing," I say. "Beautiful and ugly all at once."

"*Oui*," he says. "This is why we chose this place. For the tree."

We are in the home of an artist. Who needs the dwarves?

∽

John has been traveling the world with bass in tow for the last three decades. At the airport, some people point and stare at him. Others jump out of his way, hoping to avoid being run over by what looks like a coffin on wheels. Many feel obligated to make some sort of clever comment. "You should have played the flute" tends to top the list.

There have never been any hard rules for bassists flying with their instruments. Sometimes there's an extra charge of, say, 250 dollars. Sometimes it costs half of that. Sometimes it's free. Sometimes they won't take the bass at all.

One summer day in 1998 I'm put in charge of prechecking John's bass from Cologne to London—no small task for a woman with fragile wrists and, as a professional pianist, a genuine fear of finger injuries.

"Don't actually let them *see* the bass," John says, doing that chop-chop thing with his hands that guys do when they're giving instructions. "Park it really far away from the ticket counter, in a corner somewhere, and gesture toward it with large sweeping arm movements. Distract them—like a magician or hypnotist. And once you're checked in, tip the porter really well so he wheels the bass out of sight before they change their minds."

On the appointed day I park illegally outside of the airport terminal, unload the bass with the help of a janitor who has stepped outside for a smoke, and heave and push my way toward the British Airways check-in counter.

A woman wearing a giant backpack and pushing twins in a stroller the size of a Lexus SUV stops to open the door for me. "Wow," she says. "And I thought I had it bad."

"I should have played the flute," I say.

I park the bass about twenty yards away from the counter—halfway behind a large pillar—and get in line.

Determined to use my Girl Power to get the job done, I'm wearing a black miniskirt and too much eyeliner. Turns out the check-in person is also using her Girl Power to keep refrigerator-sized objects out of the baggage hold.

"Checking any luggage today?" she says.

"Yes," I say, using large sweeping arm movements, as previously instructed, and gesturing in the general direction of the bass.

"My God. What is *that?*"

"It's a double bass."

"Does that mean you're checking two of them?"

"No. Just one. It's a musical instrument."

"Oh. A musical instrument."

"Right. A musical instrument."

Silence. She looks at her computer monitor. "Let's see. On our list of accepted musical instruments, I have 'small bassoon'—it's obviously not that—"

"No, it's not."

"Banjo?"

"No."

"Bass trombone, cello, or contrabassoon?"

"Uh, no."

"Clarinet, French horn, flute?"

"No, no, no."

"Guitar, oboe, saxophone, or trumpet?"

"Uh—"

"Viola in a rectangular case? Violin in a shaped case? Now, which one of the instruments on the list is yours? It looks like a bass tuba to me. Or is it one of those things they play in orchestras?"

Silence. Blank stare. It's a standoff.

"It's a double bass," I say again. "It's also called a contrabass or a bass violin."

"Contrabassoon? That's on the list."

"No. Contrabass. Bassoon is a reed instrument."

Silence.

"You blow through a reed instrument. Like this."

Silence.

"The contrabass is a string instrument. With, you know, strings."

More silence. She checks her computer monitor again. "Not on the list," she says.

"Okay, some people call it an acoustic upright bass. Come on. It has to be somewhere on the list."

A sneer, a sly smile, more silence.

"So sorry. It's not on the list."

"Bass tuba wasn't on the list either, but you were willing to take it.

"No I wasn't."

"Yes you were."

"No I wasn't."

I'm starting to sweat. "Okay then, can we just *say* it's a contrabassoon?"

"So sorry, you've already told me it's a double bass, and double bass is not on our list of accepted instruments."

"Please. Can't you make an exception?"

"*No way, no how,*" she says. "That—whatever it is—is *huge*. One could sleep in there."

"Trust me, you wouldn't want to," I say. "You know, it's really much smaller than it looks."

"*No.* So sorry."

"Look, I *know* it's big, but this is really important. It's not even my instrument. I'm checking it for my husband. He has a concert in London tomorrow."

"Well, then, he should know better."

"Please,"

"NO. So sorry."

I cry, I plead, I demand to speak to the manager. It turns out she *is* the manager. I even attempt a casual bribe, flashing a few bank notes with that I'd-give-anything look. But nothing works.

Loading the bass back into the car and driving it home is bad enough. Having to admit to my husband, who is returning from a gig in Switzerland later that night, that I've failed is worse.

We don't blame the check-in people. No one teaches them about the double bass at airline school, where they are busy learning about exit-row safety procedures and gluten-free meals.

Another time a confused counter woman with a sympathetic smile decides the double bass is worth two overweight charges plus two oversize charges, a total of 300 dollars. She doesn't tag it properly, and just as John and I are boarding the plane, airport security pages him and sends him to the tarmac. In front of several scowling orange-suited baggage goons wearing padded headphones, he unpacks the bass from the fiberglass trunk and strips off the soft cover. While they poke around and search through the flight case, he does what any respectable bassist would do. He plays.

"What did you play?" I ask when he finally boards the plane.

"'Giant Steps,'" he says. "But they didn't smile or anything. Maybe they're not John Coltrane fans. They never even took off their ear protectors." But we watch them load the bass onto the plane, so he must have done something right.

There have been missed flights and missing basses. How an airline could temporarily misplace a trunk the size of a Manhattan studio apartment is beyond me, but it has happened. We have logged many hours in the baggage area designated for weird luggage—the airport black hole where the orange-suit guys deliver tranquilized puppies in kennels, racing bikes in cardboard boxes, and musical instruments too big for the conveyor belt. The bass always comes off the plane last.

$\backsim$

Several months into the bass-building project, Jean Auray sends us a photo of the curved part of the bass body resting on his worktable. The instrument, raw and relaxed, looks like a sensual and satisfied woman lying on her side, contemplating the casual miracle of the French spring. The apricot tree, flaunting green shoots that will soon burst open and protect the garden from the summer heat, peers back at the bass through the workshop window. If the bass is a woman, then this particular tree is most certainly a man.

"Wood," Jean writes, "has an intelligence of its own and amazing qualities. One just needs to listen and treat it with respect, while understanding its strengths and weaknesses. Wood is elastic, but it's solid and reactive, and capable of many sounds."

Just like a good musician.

By the time an Auray bass is finished, Jean has shaved, carved, and sanded away eighty percent of the wood. This process—bringing the instrument to life—typically takes about 400 hours. The wood must rest and dry for at least a week after each adjustment so the bass can recover.

In France, even the musical instruments get vacations.

I glance at the photo again. Under the protective gaze of the apricot tree, the half-finished bass seems to anticipate the capable hands of the French artisan and the American musician. If all goes well, they'll transform her from a silent piece of wood into an instrument that sings.

We wait. We receive more photos.

Two months later, Jean writes: "She played her first notes this afternoon. I think you will like her."

Six months after our initial meeting with M. Auray, the bass is ready. Our son is on an exchange trip to South Africa and our daughter is visiting a friend in Sicily, so John and I travel as a duo to Lyon. It's a leisurely trip, romantic even. We have just celebrated our eighteenth anniversary. That's a lot of bass. But I guess I can't get enough.

We arrive at Jean's studio, climb the now familiar steps to his workshop, and watch as he removes the finished bass from its soft cover. I'm not quite sure what to look at—the bass, the bass maker, or the bass player. All three seem locked together and suspended in the noonish August light, an impressionist painting of human accomplishment and expectation. John takes the instrument and begins to play. To a musician, this is surely one of life's most beautiful moments.

"Ah, yes," John says.

"*Oui*," says Jean.

I listen. This bass will age like a good relationship. It will open up, respond to its partner's touch, and give back everything it gets. I choke back a few tears and accompany Juliet to her kitchen to help prepare the afternoon meal. Jean and John stay in the workshop to talk and make minor adjustments.

This is the first time I've been inside the Auray living quarters. On our previous visit we were confined to the workshop. The house, on the other side of a large garage area used to store aging wood, looks like the place I dreamed of finding when I was eighteen and reading about the French countryside. It's an artisan's paradise, with handcrafted kitchen counters and cabinets, an old dining table, and scarred wooden floors. In spite of the heat, the living room is comfortable and airy, with stacks of books in the corners and a cat curled on a threadbare antique chair.

Juliet tosses a salad while I slice a baguette. She tells me about her grown children, and I talk about Curtis and Julia. When the men join us, we sit together, drink wine, and dine on melon with prosciutto, quenelles, cheese, and a sausage from a local *boucherie*. Slow food, slow talk, slow music. This is the way I want to live.

"I must go feed the pigeon," Jean says after the two-hour meal. "He fell from the sky and landed in front of our door."

"When did this happen?" I ask. I wonder if it's one of the pigeons Julia spotted six months ago.

"Yesterday," he says. "On the thirteenth. We have named him Treize." Jean grabs an eyedropper from a drawer. "I think Treize will be with us for a while. Right now he lives in a modified box, but soon I will be conducting the exercise class for him. I will throw him in the air, and he will fly. But maybe he will stay awhile and live in the apricot tree."

"If I were Treize I would never leave this place," I say.

We tour the garden, see the pond where Jean likes to swim in the afternoons after he has finished his day's work, and retreat to the workshop where John learns how to dismantle the bass and pack it into the *Nanoo* flight case.

"Remember," says Jean. "At the airport you should call her the *cello-bass*."

We're not flying today, we're driving, and we must leave if we want to miss the *autoroute* traffic. John begins packing the instrument into the *Nanoo* for the trip home. Before he closes the case, Jean Auray rests his hand on the bass for a moment.

"It must be hard to say goodbye," I say.

"I like to start anew again and again," says Jean. "It's my way of moving forward, not to get in a rut, a kind of challenge in the face of time—"

"I will take care of her," says John.

"Please," says Jean.

As we drive away, Jean stands by the front door, waving. It's a sight I will never forget, the luthier releasing his work of art into the wild.

The transfer from one artist to the other is complete.

Turn right at the next intersection, says Kate.

"Turn that thing off," says John. "I know where I'm going."

The House on Sorority Row

S isters in life, sisters in death.

I was one of the lead actresses cast in the 1983 Film Ventures chop-up-the-college-girls cult classic *The House on Sorority Row*. Fans of the film may remember me as the clumsy and idiotic blond who grabs a butcher knife, runs down a hallway while being chased by an invisible killer (later revealed to be a schizophrenic clown), trips and falls, and—here's the idiotic part—*hides in the bathroom*, where she meets her shocking fate.

Slasher Film 101: Never ever hide in the bathroom.

I'm thinking about this now, because this week—twenty-six years after the debut of the original film—*Sorority Row* premieres again, this time around as a "contemporary horror film" with a new cast, including Carrie "Princess Leia" Fisher (daughter of Eddie Fisher and Debbie Reynolds), Rumer Willis (daughter of Bruce Willis and Demi Moore), and a handful of unknown but undoubtedly hopeful and hardworking actresses. I wonder what each of them had to go through to get the job. I suspect the audition game is much the same as it was for me all those years ago. I'm lucky I escaped that phase of my life with my head on straight. Almost.

In the eighties I lived in New York City but paid my rent—and my dues—by playing the piano at the Waterbury, Connecticut, Holiday Inn, home of the all-you-can-eat Scampi Buffet, the Blue

Hawaiian two-for-one cocktail hour, a spinet piano with a missing leg, and a handful of semi-toothless customers with names like Clarkie, Dutch, and Roy-Boy. Playing the piano in a seedy cocktail bar motivated me to keep striving for higher levels of employment. I loved making music, but I had stars in my eyes, a college degree in drama, and big ideas about the limelight, motion pictures, and serious acting. I read about the open auditions for *The House on Sorority Row* in an actor's trade publication called *Backstage*. Anxious for a chance to escape Waterbury, I decided to go, even though I knew it would be the ultimate cattle call.

Almost 700 actresses showed up to audition for seven roles— a throbbing mass of female talent squashed into a tiny Midtown rehearsal-studio lobby. We were a perfumed blob of blind faith, giddy optimism, and desperation, up to our layered bangs in apricot blush and lash-plumping mascara. Twenty-five years later, I'm sure some jaded but curious janitorial team is still scraping glitter gel, nail-polish claw marks, and lipstick stains off the walls. Revlon Perfect Pink, with just a hint of shimmer.

There were over 650 rejects that day, which might have been a record, even for New York City.

❧

Needle-fine April drizzle splatters my forehead as I cross Fifty-fifth Street. Springtime in New York: Pedestrians leap over puddles, and the air smells like a noxious broth of exhaust fumes and clean linen. I join the conga line of actresses coiling past the rehearsal-studio door and worry that the humidity will ruin my makeup.

"You're number 430," says a know-it-all manboy with a whiny voice. "Wait for your number to be called."

The young women assembled are a lush bunch, with cranked-up hair, strappy high heels, and tight synthetic sweaters in earthy colors. Most of these ladies have model potential—chiseled faces and perfect bodies—but they're two or three inches too short for a career in fashion. It's a room jam-packed with Elite Model spit-backs—gorgeous but slightly squat.

At an open casting call, when this many actors show up for so few roles, the casting director does something called "typing." Here's how it goes: Ten nervous wannabes are herded into a fluorescent-lit room. They stand there like iced cupcakes in a bakery window while the casting director looks them over once or twice. Several of the original ten are given a "callback," or an invitation to return, with slightly better odds. The casting director, often a woman with a sad smile and a ratty black pantsuit, mutters a hurried *thank you for your time* and glances at her oversized watch. Then she herds the rejects out of the room by holding open the door and shouting—through a fake smile with clenched teeth—*NEXT, PLEASE* into the waiting area. The dejected group shuffles out, a hopeful group bounces in. It's like two forces of life, pulling and pushing at the same vague promise.

I figure it might take several hours before the casting director gets to my group. No chairs left, so I sit on the floor and try not to think about soiling my best coat. A pitted path in the grubby linoleum leads from the lobby into the casting area, probably from decades of stiletto heels digging into the spongy surface.

I scope out the cupcake competition and listen to the chatter.

"Do I look fat?"

"No."

My puffy face depresses me; most of my 125 pounds is located above my neck. But because it's chilly outside and raining sideways, and because I have a stale street-vendor pretzel and a thermos of coffee in my bag, and because I don't have anywhere else to go until the bus leaves for Waterbury, I decide to stay and devise a strategy. Maybe the Paul Mitchell hair-spray fumes will help me think.

An idea hits me. Horror films are formula films. There's always an awkward girl, an unfortunate-looking sidekick, an ugly duckling. This could be me—the dweeb. Because I have my Waterbury overnight bag with me, I've got access to a large supply of ugly-girl enhancement tools: makeup remover, hair twisties, pink Keds, fat-girl sweat pants, reading glasses, and a baggy old T-shirt. I shove my way into the crowded bathroom, where I change clothes and experiment with some bad-posture poses. An hour later the man-boy calls my group into the studio. While my beautiful competitors fluff their hair and beam at the casting director as if they're auditioning for a Pantene commercial, I stare at my feet.

"Pathetic," says the casting lady.

"I know," says a Jesus-looking man standing in the corner. "She's perfect."

The Jesus look-alike strolls over to me and introduces himself. "I'm Mark Rosman, the director. I think you're my Jeanie."

"The rest of you, thank you very much." The casting lady wedges open the door with her boot. "NEXT PLEASE!" she yells into the crowded lobby.

I shake hands with Jesus, make an appointment to read for him, and slip out the door as the next group of calendar girls sashays in. I haven't yet been offered the part, but somehow I know I've nailed it.

I float—*float!*—to the Port Authority to catch the bus to Waterbury, where I play that evening for two mentally challenged people named Dennis and Maryanne. They get completely pissed drinking two-for-one Blue Hawaiians, argue at top volume, and then throw Pepperidge Farm Goldfish at each other, but I don't care, not one bit, because I have a shot at an acting job in a real movie, and soon, very soon, I'll be out of the Waterbury Holiday Inn. Who knows where *The House on Sorority Row* might take me?

∾

Five days later I return to Manhattan for my callback, where I read several scenes, most of which include references to blood, guts, and a murdered housemother bobbing in an algae-filled swimming pool.

"Would you please scream for me, Robin?" asks Jesus.

"Why, of course," I say. "Uh—you might want to cover your ears." I let it rip.

"Thank you. Very passionate, very heartfelt, very loud—just what I'm looking for. Many of your scenes will be without much dialogue, either because you'll be in the process of being murdered or you'll already be dead."

"Can't talk when you're dead."

"Exactly, because you're, well, dead! You get it! Let's try another scene, this time with some tears." He shuffles through a stack of pages.

"But you can't cry when—"

"Here!" He hands me a sheet of paper with one word on it: *HELP*. "You're in a desperate situation. You scream for help, then you cry hysterically. Got it?"

"Got it. Wait! Am I dead?"

"Not yet. Got it?"

"Got it."

Scream. Cry. Scream. Cry. Eat a tuna sandwich, drink coffee out of the blue-and-white paper cup. Start all over again. Scream. Scream. Louder.

"One more time, please, this time for the camera."

We finish the day with me crying for about twenty minutes. I'm good at crying on cue. Salty tears. Big ones, the kind that plop on the floor and almost make a sound.

∽

"Congratulations, Robin," says the production manager, a sturdy guy with a lopsided smile. "The role of Jeanie is yours."

Finally. A part in a movie!

"You'll start shooting on July 1st, with several days of costume shopping and makeup tests ahead of time. Oh, you'll have to be fitted for your neck prosthesis next week."

Neck prosthesis? At this point I haven't seen the complete script. This prosthesis word makes me nervous.

"We'll pay you fifty dollars a day on days that you work. Plus travel expenses and housing."

That's all? I earn way more than that in Waterbury. How will I cover my rent?

Robert checks his clipboard. "You are fifth to die in the film, and then, let's see here, you come back as a zombie and as a head in the toilet, so you'll have a lot to do."

"A head in the toilet? *My* head in the toilet?"

"Chopped off, of course. It's really the highlight of the entire film. The pinnacle of the dramatic curve."

"Oh. How will you—"

"And we'll provide meals and housing and transportation from New York City to Baltimore. A driver will pick you up at the train station and take you to the hospice."

"The *hospice?*"

"Whoops, silly me. I mean the hostel. I always get those words mixed up. You'll be staying at a *hostel* that usually houses Sufi dancers. Community bathroom, but you'll have your own bedroom. You'll have to bring your own sheets and towels."

❦

A week later I find myself in the special-effects guy's Brooklyn brownstone, with my face and neck submerged in a bucket of high-tech gunk, the plastery material used to cast wax figures of Nelson Mandela and Elizabeth Taylor for Madame Tussaud's Wax Museum. I breath through a wide straw and try not to panic.

"Gorgeous, Robin, gorgeous!" he says to my bucket-covered head. "This will be beautiful! I'm going to mold some torn tendons and severed arteries for this baby. Lots of gory details. It'll be fabulous!" My ears are partially submerged, so his voice sounds muffled, as if he were talking through Jell-O.

I grunt a reply through the straw: "Forfffowwwffong?"

"Just a few minutes longer," he says. "And then we'll get you out of that bucket. Sorry I'm dunking your face in there, but I have to make a mold of it to get the proper neck dimensions."

On the bus ride back to Waterbury, somewhere around Danbury, I figure out I won't be able to give up my piano gig—*Sorority Row* won't pay enough. It's a classic New York predicament. I'll have to stay out of town earning money to pay for an empty apartment.

I won't be home for weeks at a time. Shit. I notice something funny in my ear—a glob of dried pink plaster.

I play my Friday-night set, stopping every so often to pick little pieces of goo out of my hair. I plink out a Gershwin medley and think about the plaster replica of my face and neck floating in a toilet bowl. Clarkie, Dutch, and Roy-Boy drink their blue drinks and stare at the ceiling all night, occasionally taking a moment to yell out a word spelled backwards, an activity they enjoy.

"*Nibor!*"

"*Onaip!*"

I brush cigarette ashes off the keyboard, play "Embraceable You," and wonder how I'll manage to do both gigs. Shit.

Gig spelled backwards is still gig.

There's an old joke: How do you get an actress to complain? Give her a job.

There's another old joke: How do you get a musician to complain? Give her a job.

∽

Harley, Eileen, Kathy, Jodie, Ellen, Janis, and I—the lucky seven actresses playing the unlucky seven sorority sisters—meet in Pikesville, Maryland, a few days before shooting begins. Costume shopping turns gloomy when I realize the other actresses will be wearing sexy evening dresses, bikinis, and cutoff shorts (standard slasher-film attire), but I, the cast misfit, will be dressed in the college-girl equivalent of Garanimals—mix-and-match polyester outfits with color-coordinated bows for my hair. One scene calls for baby-blue overalls that make me look slightly pregnant.

Most of the film will be shot in a rambling Pikesville mansion that has been art-directed to look like a ritzy sorority house and dormitory. Everything is fake, but familiar in a funky way, and I feel as if I've been zapped back to college days. There are big plastic containers of half-used cosmetics in the bathroom, Bruce Springsteen posters on the doors, and threadbare oriental rugs in the library. Bright, airy, warm, dormy. Fake.

In reverse-Technicolor contrast, the house the film company has rented from the Sufis is all too real. It's a hostile hostel where we will hang out and sleep for the duration of the shoot. It's grimy, spooky, and home to most of the Pikesville bat population. At unannounced times dozens of bearded men in long white robes inhabit the main living room. They spin and spin and spin in silent circles with their arms held up to the filthy ceiling, praising heaven, praising Pikesville, perfecting the art of spinning in place.

While the Sufis dance my sisters and I hide in the community kitchen, gorging on Archway cookies, Entenmann's fudge cake, and take-out pepperoni pizza, wondering if we'll look fat in the next day's rushes. From the beginning of time, this is how actresses have bonded.

"Do I look fat?"

"No. Do I?"

"No, are you crazy? Have some more cake. It's raspberry-lemon-lite, and besides, you need the energy for your big scene tomorrow—it'll be, like, really emotionally draining."

An ancient upright grand piano, almost in tune, stands in one of the back rooms. Sometimes, after a careful check for wandering Sufis and Grandpa Munster–sized bats hanging from the eaves, I go in there and play. One or two of the sisters join me, and together we sing Billy Joel songs about getting high, aiming low, and clinging to past regrets. We're way too young to sing such songs, but we pretend to understand the lyrics.

❧

Now that I have the job, Director Mark has stopped reminding me of Jesus. On the first day of shooting he greets us with a description of the plot: "Here's how it goes: The Evil Housemother—who hates every single one of you— catches Eileen doing the nasty-nasty in her sorority-girl waterbed. The Evil Housemother slashes the waterbed—whoosh!—with her silver-tipped Evil Cane and completely ruins Eileen's romantic moment by knocking her and her boyfriend out of their passionate embrace. The scene concludes with poor Eileen shivering on the flooded bedroom floor, plotting to take revenge on the Evil Housemother."

❧

"Well, ladies, I held my ground," says Eileen after her waterbed scene. "I absolutely refused to show my breasts."

Eileen's bedroom scene has been shot on a closed set—restricted to anyone but the necessary crew—and we've spent much of the morning speculating about what might be going on in there.

"I stayed 100 percent *fully clothed*," she says.

"Did anyone see my striped kneesocks?" asks Harley. "I can't find them anywhere, and my feet are freezing."

One year later, at the premiere of *The House on Sorority Row*, we'll see Eileen on the silver screen, wearing nothing but those kneesocks. The stripes add a nice touch.

❧

Director Mark: "For revenge, the sisters play a prank on the Evil Housemother. Eileen threatens the housemother with a gun just to make a point and scare her, but—BOOM!—the gun accidentally goes off, and she shoots—and kills—the housemother. The old lady tumbles into the swimming pool, blood pours out of her huge chest, and her corpse is floating there in the bloody water. The special-effects guy has a blood pump you won't believe. The girls, anxious to hide their crime before the big sorority-house party starts, drag her out of the water, put her in a sack with rocks, and roll her back into the pool. She sinks to the bottom. But the main thing is—and this is the beauty part—everyone thinks the Evil Housemother is dead and gone, which is actually true! But when the girls start dying, the audience will believe the housemother has somehow gotten out of that pool to murder them! And, get this, the girls all show up in the pool later in the film, after they're all dead. How cool is that?"

The prop master handles the gun with care, but still, it's unsettling to be around Eileen with a real Glock 42 in her manicured hands. My character is supposed to be nervous, so I bite my nails and twitch just a tad more.

"Too much makeup on Robin," says Director Mark. "She looks too glamorous."

"I look like a squirrel." I'm sitting between Ellen, who looks like Audrey Hepburn, and Harley, who's a ringer for Lauren Bacall. Back in the wardrobe area, the makeup artist removes my lip gloss and accentuates the circles under my eyes, while the costume lady adjusts my Garanimals overalls and fusses with my hair ribbons. Turns out to be just as much work to make an actress look bad as it is to make her look good. Almost.

"Perfect," says Director Mark. "Now let's murder the housemother."

Fine. We shoot the housemother, push her into the pool, and watch her body sink. Director Mark wraps for the day. To celebrate, we eat piles of bagels and feed scraps of boiled ham to Rocket the dog, a three-legged mutt who hangs out on the set. Then we return to House o' Sufi, rummage through the kitchen in search of old cake, and watch the turbaned men spin.

"Do I look fat?"

"No."

Later that night I hear sex noises coming from some of my sisters' rooms. Maybe a Sufi or two has whirled up the back stairs, or maybe a lighting technician or production assistant has sneaked in the back door. I squeeze my eyes shut and try not to care. I dream of kneesocks and Dutch and Roy-Boy, and of sitting on the edge of a Jell-O–filled swimming pool while everyone else jumps in and swims.

Nibor!

∽

We put her back in the pool and she was still *alive*, emotes Kathy, the big star of the film, also known as The Girl Who Lives. The entire plot depends on the audience believing that the Evil Housemother has gotten out of her rock-filled sack at the bottom of the pool and returned to the sorority house to start knocking us off with her Evil Cane.

Ellen is murdered in the basement, with a haunting silhouette of her perfectly pert profile projected onto a stone wall by a lone lightbulb that loops back and forth. The Evil Cane lunges into the frame and, *ploomp*, stabs her in the throat.

"Gruesome, but tasteful," we tell each other.

"Director Mark is really good."

"Yeah, he's like Hitchcock. He knows how to tell a story with style. Like, *artisticfully*, you know?"

"Did I look fat?"

"No."

Jodie, who probably isn't as dumb as she looks, but still, I have to wonder, buys it at the base of the attic steps. The attic-cam rushes toward her open mouth and frozen platinum hair and leaves her demise to our imaginations. I like to think she dies because she swallows the camera. She also does not look fat.

Never ever go near the attic.

Janis never reveals her real name. She's a thirty-five-year-old actress with an actual career who has decided to accept a role as a college girl in a slasher film rather than spend the summer serving nachos in a Malibu restaurant. The killer snags Janis while she's snooping around the basement looking for Ellen.

Horror Film + Basement = Bad News.

Harley Jane Kozak is my favorite of the seven sisters, mainly because she wears Army-surplus Bermuda shorts, always has a good book in her hands, and teaches me how to French-braid my hair. A gloved hand grabs her while she is poking around in the bushes looking for clues.

Never ever poke around in the bushes.

Eileen falls into an open grave, breasts first. Really, if you're going to die, it's convenient to do it right over a hole in the ground. When I see the rushes I'm impressed with Eileen's death throes;

she even takes a moment to fix her hair while she's falling. And she absolutely, 100 percent, positively does not look fat.

If you want to stay alive, never *hang out in the cemetery, especially if you're wearing a halter top.*

The half-drowned housemother is a true menace, and Director Mark is milking each death scene to its fullest potential.

"But, you know, he does it so tastefully."

The killer catches up with me—Jeanie—at the back gate to the sorority house.

Always use the front door. Never go through the back gate.

After grappling with the mystery killer and the Evil Cane, I escape, run into the kitchen, and lock the door behind me. I rummage through a drawer, pull out a machete-sized butcher knife, then sit there nervously and wait for something to happen. Stupid really, because everyone knows that if you sit and wait, the killer shows up and you're in deep shit. But I'm not the writer. I'm just the actress hired to play the stupid girl. So I wait.

༄

Director Mark: "Here's where things get interesting. The sorority girls are gurking, one at a time, all over the house. Poor little Jeanie is sitting alone in the kitchen, just waitin' to meet her maker. There are loads of teenagers at the party in the next room. Jeanie could go in there, get the band to stop playing that god-awful music, and call the police, but no, she sits there like an idiot with the butcher knife in her hands. The killer rattles the door to the kitchen, and then—smash!—the Evil Cane breaks through the glass window. Jeanie races up the back stairway, clutching the butcher knife. She runs down the hallway, bouncin' off the walls, slippin' and slidin' on the slick sorority-house floor.

"And then she falls—splat! She cuts herself with the knife, sees the dribbles of blood on her yellow dress, and feels sick to her stomach. We can hear the killer coming, faster and faster. But Jeanie thinks she might throw up, so she runs into the bathroom where she can vomit in private. I know what you're thinking: No, no, no! Not the bathroom! Why the bathroom? I will tell you why: Jeanie might be stupid, but she's a lady to the end. No way would she toss her cookies right there in the hallway. I wouldn't want to portray her in any other way, except like really dignified."

⁂

"Cut!" Director Mark yells. "We've got a situation. Someone deal with the knife situation, please!"

The rubber prop knife doesn't look authentic, so Director Mark opts for a real butcher knife. Blunt, but still. The trick is to release the knife as I fall, thereby avoiding a real-life self-stabbing incident that would seriously jeopardize the plot but ultimately be great for the tabloids and trade rags. Flinging the knife endangers the technicians who are racing backwards on a dolly track in a very narrow hallway. One bad knife toss and I could take out half of the crew. I feign a couple of threatening moves toward the Best Boy, just to keep him on his toes. If I'm only making $50 a day, what's that poor guy making? I practice running and falling without my weapon until I feel comfortable enough to add the knife to my choreographed routine of *run, fall, gag*. After nineteen takes, the repair of a cluster of open blisters on my sandal-clad feet caused by the Payless white plastic sandals that were not made for stuntwomen, and injuries that will result in humongo purple bruises on both knees, I get it just right. I finish the take, crawl into the bathroom while making gagging noises, and the entire crew claps for me.

The next day I return to Waterbury to play a weekend's worth of piano gigs. Compared to House o' Sufi, the Holiday Inn looks like the Waldorf Astoria. I greet Dennis and Maryanne as if they're my long-lost retarded relatives. I even sit at the bar next to Dutch and Roy-Boy and compliment them on their matching plaid flannel shirts. I wear a long evening dress to cover my bruises and—in between sets of Janis Ian tunes and Beatles hits— I tell my coworkers complete lies about my glamorous life as an actress.

The next bit, my big death scene in the dormitory bathroom, is scheduled for the following week at the Baltimore Public High School for Performing Arts.

∾

Director Mark: "The killer enters the bathroom and we see poor Jeanie, crouched up on the toilet seat like a little rabbit, nibbling on her fingernails, holding her butcher knife, and saying her prayers, hoping the Good Lord or someone will see fit to spare her pathetic life, even if she is wearing such an awful dress. The killer turns on the showers, and steam fills the room.

"Very scary. Jeanie hears the first toilet stall door open, then the second. She's in stall number three. We wait. We wait. We wait.

"Whack! The Evil Cane breaks the lock on Jeanie's toilet stall. Scream, scream, scream! As the killer pushes her up against the white wall, a gloved hand comes into the frame and forces Jeanie's neck up against the blade of her very own knife. Squirt, squirt, squirt, out comes the blood. Red on white. Very dramatic. This'll be great, great, great.

"Gurk, gurk, gurk, down goes Jeanie, with one hand clawing—think chalkboard noise here—at the stall wall, the other hand holding onto the very knife that's taking off her head.

"I want people to taste irony in Jeanie's death. If only she'd stayed out of that bathroom. If only she'd let go of that knife. If only, if only. But, you know, for the sake of the plot, she's gotta die."

❧

"Cue steam! Cue blood!" Director Mark shouts. He shoots my death scene without sound, which allows him to yell verbal cues at me while we're filming. "Okay, Robin, you're really scared. Now you're *really really* scared. Now you hear that first door open and you're even more scared."

He also cues the effects people. "More steam—get it to waft in her face, force the door open. Whack her with the cane. Careful the point doesn't poke her eye out! Knife to her neck! Blood pump, blood pump, blood pump, *pump, pump, pump! Now, now, now!*

This blood pump is a big drag. It's attached to a hose that snakes under my Garanimals dress and ends right at the base of my skull. The special-effects man, who's becoming my least favorite person on the set, squats on the floor underneath me, and when he receives his cue—*blood!*—he pushes down a plunger that forces the fake blood through the hose and out of the nozzle by my head. The fake blood looks real—it even smells real—and I wonder if the special-effects guy is copping it from a pig farm not too far from House o' Sufi. But I'm a professional actress, and I soldier on without asking questions. In between takes I scrub off the pig blood, change into a new version of my dress, eat Fig Newtons, and lie on the lavatory floor staring up at the institutional-white ceiling.

Never once does it occur to me to quit.

"Once more, Robin, then we'll have it. Cue steam. Cue blood pump. Action."

Twelve hours of work, three different setups, five takes with a knife at my throat, and I'm finally dead.

෧෨

Director Mark: "But she's not dead! That's the genius of this script. You think the girls are dead, but they come back. They come back as zombies! They float in the swimming pool! And then, and then, and then— get this—we see the head. We see, for a split second, poor little Jeanie's head floating in the toilet bowl. What a thing. It will look 100 percent real."

෧෨

"In there? I have to stick my head in there? Is that a real toilet?"

"Yes, but we cleaned it thoroughly."

I knew they would be shooting footage of my actual head with a fake neck glued to it, but I never thought they would make me put my head inside an actual toilet. It has taken the effects team hours to glue the prosthesis to my neck and apply my dead person makeup. Now I'm supposed to sit *underneath* the floor of a fake toilet stall—built on a platform—and stick my real head and fake neck through a hole cut in the bottom of the porcelain bowl. The cameraman will be on a ladder above me, on the platform, shooting down.

A production assistant guides my head into the hole. I have a rather large head for a woman who is by no means fat, and this is a small hole, so we use a wedge-and-shove technique to get both my head and the prosthesis inside the toilet. Someone shoves a barstool under my butt so I can sit, but the stool is too low, and my neck—

the real one, not the fake one—wrenches. I look up and see Director Mark smiling down at me.

"You look great!"

"Shit," I say, losing my cool. "I can't do this."

"Sure you can," he says. "It's the movies. Got it?"

"Got it. But. Hurry. And could someone scratch my nose?"

"Something doesn't look quite right in the toilet bowl," says the special-effects man. "Throw some water in there." Six or seven people stand above me on the platform. One of them holds a bucket.

What would Meryl do?

"And we need to mix some blood with the water."

Pig blood?

"Could you please hurry?"

"Let's start rolling," says Director Mark. "Hang in there, Robin."

"Head to the side, head straight. More blood on her neck. More water in her face. Eyes closed. Eyes open. Makeup! Wipe away the tears! Come on, Robin, get it together—dead people don't cry!"

"Yes they do," I shout.

Three hours later he has his shot.

It takes half a bottle of spirit gum remover and twenty minutes of scrubbing in the shower to remove the prosthesis. Pig blood or fake blood, whatever it is, it leaves an ugly stain.

"Here, Robin." The special-effects guy hands me the gunky prosthesis like he's presenting an Oscar. "I want you to have this."

"Fuck you," I say. I throw his fake neck at him and leave to get the train back to Waterbury. I need a piano, a Blue Hawaiian, and a dose of reality.

∽

The Waterbury gig ends a few months later. Dutch has died—a real death, not a fake one—and Roy-Boy and Clarkie have drifted away. I begin to get piano work in Manhattan.

The following year my fake sorority sisters and I attend a New York City premiere of the movie. What fun we have. We giggle when we see a topless Eileen wearing Harley's long-lost kneesocks, we scream at the shot of my head in the toilet, we give ourselves a standing ovation as the credits roll. Then, before we say goodbye forever, we go to a party and tell each other how beautiful and thin we are. *The House on Sorority Row* is a huge hit with slasher-film fans, a group that's larger than one might hope. Since the movie features the creative demise of seven rich white girls, it also develops a cult following of ethnic minority teenagers. I'm recognized on the subway for several months after the premiere.

"Hey, lady, aren't you the head in the toilet?"

"Yes."

"You're some kind of bad, lady."

"Thank you," I say, because that's what Meryl would do.

Not one of the original seven sisters, not even The Girl Who Lived, was asked to appear as a zombie, a ghost, or a head in the toilet in the new big-budget version of *The House on Sorority Row*. Any one of us could have played the Evil Housemother, but that role went to Carrie Fisher, herself no stranger to horror-film scenarios, although I doubt she ever sat next to Roy-Boy in the Waterbury Holiday Inn or ducked a flying mammal at the House o' Sufi.

I still haven't seen the remake.

Mark Rosman continues to direct films. I imagine him at casting calls, pulling the pathetic girl out of the lineup and giving her a job because he knows she won't quit, no matter what. He knows she wants to be in the movies. She'll respect his judgment and trust his instincts. And he will coax her to put her head in the toilet, to take off her bra, to cry on cue, to run with a weapon or dive into a pool full of muck. She will follow through. *Artisticfully.*

Almost three decades ago, we—the seven actresses—hoped to escape our jobs as waitresses, office workers, and piano players in cheesy bars. After the *Sorority Row* premiere was over and the hoopla had fizzled, we drifted away from each other, betting our careers would someday offer more than an Evil Cane and a dunk in an algae-filled pool. Eileen, Kathy, and Harley have had lovely careers doing projects that did not, to my knowledge, involve pig blood or Sufi dancers. We're also mothers and wives and tenders of homes, gardens, and patchwork careers. Even though we've reinvented ourselves countless times, I'm guessing that, even now, we are not fat.

Sisters in life, sisters in death. We were some kind of bad. On that cattle-call day in 1982, my hair stiff with cherry-scented mousse, I thought a role in a movie would change everything about my life. In a way, it did. I wonder if somewhere in that old Fifty-fifth Street rehearsal studio traces of my face powder still linger—Max Factor Glow Girl, in Frosted Rosé. The company discontinued the color years ago, but it was a lovely shade.

The Piano Teacher

William Chrystal taught hundreds of piano students during his lifetime. I was lucky enough to be one of them.

I'm four decades and an ocean away from the time and place of my first piano lesson, but I remember a handful of details: the stone steps that led from McCully Street to Mr. Chrystal's home in the Mt. Lebanon section of Pittsburgh, the grayish-green color of the carpeting in his studio, the enormous grand pianos sitting side by side like twin ebony ships ready to sail, the pungent smell of his hair tonic, the way his glasses always seemed a little foggy.

As I sat in Mr. Chrystal's light-filled studio and waited for my lesson to begin, the silence sometimes seemed dense enough to slice. But then the door would creak, and he would enter the room and go to his Steinway—either to show me how a particular passage was supposed to sound or to accompany one of my stuttering attempts to make sense of the mess of notes in front of me—and the air would grow crisp, almost brittle with possibility. Teaching a child to play the piano is a fragile process; it involves transferring, little by little, the weight of too much information onto the bony shoulders of a child's undefined dreams.

Mr. Chrystal began playing the piano when he was four years old. He practiced and practiced, becoming an accomplished musician long before he finished high school. By the time he graduated from the Peabody School of Music in Baltimore—with the coveted Artist Diploma—he had earned a reputation as an excellent concert pianist and formidable teacher. He issued commands, he made demands; he had sharpshooter musical focus and long-distance-runner discipline. He expected his students to develop the same practice habits that had launched his career. He wanted us to *get it right.*

I hardly ever got it right. As a kid I left my dresser drawers open, I wore mismatched socks, I tried to bake cakes without recipes and make model airplanes without instructions. I lost important papers and the kitchen scissors, made good use of my shortcut gene to fudge my way through most academic pursuits, and once, determined to be an Olympic gymnast, tried to do a split without any training. *Getting it right* was never high on my list of priorities. Today I'm a competent writer and musician, but only because Mr. Chrystal, a million years ago, convinced me that the serious study of music had nothing in common with my free-spirit approach to nearly everything else.

Fly or fall. With the wrong teacher, a child's musical development can hydroplane, jackknife, and end up abandoned in a broken heap on the side of the road. With the right teacher and a healthy amount of inspired practice, a little girl might eventually learn enough about music to help her cope with a decidedly unmusical world. I didn't realize it at the time, but Bill Chrystal was the right teacher for me. He refused to allow my ditzy side to participate in those early years of study, because I had technique to learn. It was his job to teach it to me and my job to practice until I got it right. We had an unspoken agreement—if we both did our parts, I would not end up as artistic roadkill.

"Music is peculiar," he used to say. "It takes fifteen years of hard work to find out whether or not you can play." All these years later I understand what he meant. A child can't exercise her talent if she never takes the time to learn the technique. It often takes more than a decade just to reach an acceptable level of competence, a level that allows a player's artistry to break through the layers of technique, a level that allows a teenage musician to figure out who she is.

The precision Mr. Chrystal required nearly drove me crazy. Often no amount of practice would suffice. Sometimes I wanted to quit. Daggers darted at me from behind his misty glasses, and he snarled whenever I stumbled over a phrase, or, worse yet, forgot the fingering pattern he had already circled in red pencil. Red pencil markings came first, then, if I repeated the same mistake at the next lesson, he used his blue pencil. Third time? He slammed the music book shut and dismissed me until I could come back and play the phrase. *Perfectly*. Get it right, or not at all.

The only student who escaped Mr. Chrystal's judgmental stare was Stephen Flaherty, who went on to a spectacular career as a Broadway and film composer. Boy Wonder Stephen began showing up at Mr. Chrystal's student-only repertory classes when I was in my teens. Twelve years old at the time, Stephen was tiny in stature, with an unusual amount of poise and precision in his playing. He didn't wear glasses, but he did look a little like Mr. Chrystal, who would sit in the audience during Stephen's performances and glow with pride. The rest of us, the great unwashed of the piano-student world, would receive a withering stare, a cringing half-grin, or a threatening shake of his head.

At the end of each repertory class, Mr. Chrystal's first wife, a Southern belle whose name really was Elizabeth Taylor, would serve us cookies and punch. Mr. Chrystal would sip a martini. On the rocks.

There were times I hated him.

"With your limited technique," he once said to me, "you would be better off in woodshop class somewhere, building knickknack shelves that no one will ever use."

Perhaps I was suffering from a piano-student version of the Stockholm syndrome—the captive falling for the captor—but I loved him, too. I loved him when he smiled, just a little, and said, after one of my nerve-jangled attempts to play Debussy, "not bad." I loved him—and more important, I believed him—when he told me I might have a future as a songwriter. And I loved him most of all whenever I heard him in concert. He was a small man, but onstage he seemed huge, puffed up, seven feet tall. His performing spirit, which he kept under cover in his teaching studio, always surprised me when he stepped onstage. He had two personalities: his take-no-prisoners teacher side, and his other, more artistic character, the one that shaped his playing. That's a funny word—*play*. It takes a lot of hard work before you earn the right to play. He liked to remind me of that.

Mr. Chrystal played with the Pittsburgh Symphony under William Steinberg. He was on the faculty of Carnegie Mellon University and Chatham College. He played with the Pittsburgh Ballet and the Civic Light Opera, and he was a guest soloist with other symphony orchestras in the area. And he was my teacher. For one hour every week, he belonged to me. For a dozen years our relationship stayed exactly the same. I would practice, never enough. Thursday afternoons would find me with a nervous stomach, worried that I would once again fall short of his expectations.

We did our best not to give up on each other.

Several years after his marriage to Elizabeth Taylor ended, and long before he met Annie Trager, the woman who would become the love of his life, Mr. Chrystal had a romantic relationship with a college roommate of mine, Peg, who was twenty-four years younger than he was. Peg, an intellectual young woman with a wicked sense of humor and a truckload of artistic and academic talent, had met Bill in a college musical-theater course. I was never comfortable around the two of them. I was still studying with him, he still intimidated me, and it didn't seem quite right to hang out with him on a double date and call him "Bill." We'd sit in a Squirrel Hill restaurant called Sodini's while Peg and I tried to act older, Bill tried to act younger, and we all tried to be hip by drinking martinis and eating funky veal dishes with tomato sauce and telling stupid-musician jokes, mostly about singers. But even with younger-than-spring Peg at his side, I felt edgy around him. I knew those blue and red pencils were just under his suit jacket, and I kept waiting for him to yank them out and start circling the mistakes I was making in real life. I was twenty years old at the time. I made a lot of mistakes.

Peg eventually left Bill and went to Oxford, where she met her future husband. I eventually left Pittsburgh, moved to New York City, and built a knickknack shelf of a career for myself as a hotel pianist, lyricist, and author of books about music. I still wonder how far I might have gotten if I had remembered to sit up straighter and curve my fingers a little more.

Bill Chrystal's words to me over the years helped carve my career. I avoided the concert stage and limited my musical pursuits to background-music jobs because he told me I would never be a great pianist and I believed him. On the other hand, I continued writing, both music and words, because he suggested I had potential and I trusted him. He pointed a light at a path and I followed it. I wish I could have let him know how well it has all worked out, but it's only now, forty-plus years after that first terrifying climb up the steps to his studio, that I realize how he continues to influence my life's work.

Bill Chrystal died on Friday, August 29, 2008. I've never been sure of the proper etiquette for informing ex-lovers about the death of an old flame, but when I received the news, I figured I ought to call Peg and let her know. We had been out of touch for several years, but we picked up like we had never stopped sitting on our carpeted dorm-room floor, legs tucked beneath us, sipping hot chocolate from chipped mugs. We had a good long-distance cry, not necessarily for Bill, but for ourselves, the fly-by years, the songs we used to sing and play, the silly punchlines that still made us laugh, the girls in their twenties we still claimed to be. I remembered my time with Bill as challenging and terrifying. She remembered her time with him as challenging and wonderful.

A week after our phone conversation she wrote to me: "Bill had a sort of professional elegance, combined with personal impatience, that made people pay attention, and also made those who studied and performed with him work harder to be better."

In her letter Peg also recalled phoning the rehearsal hall at the Civic Light Opera and asking for Bill during a break in the rehearsal of *Oklahoma*. Margaret Hamilton—yes, the Wicked Witch of the West from *The Wizard of Oz*—answered. Before she passed the phone to Bill, she said to Peg, "Let me tell you—Bill Chrystal is great!"

"So there you are," wrote Peg. "The Wicked Witch herself was suitably impressed."

❧

I'd love to know exactly how many students passed through that McCully Street door, and what became of each of them. Both of my children take weekly piano lessons—from a gentle and talented German music teacher named Thomas Lehn—and as I watch them grapple with their assignments, as I listen to them practice and struggle to *get it right*, I understand a little more about Bill Chrystal's methods. Like any good piano teacher, he taught his students to tame life's chaos by conquering the tricky musical passages he assigned to us. Maybe in our playing he heard the sound of hope—not the smooth-edged hope of easy optimism, but hard-earned hope, the kind that comes from blending determination with dreams.

Bill Chrystal taught me that music gives back whatever I put into it. Music is an art that cannot be mastered, but joy—along with a healthy dose of frustration—awaits anyone who is willing to try. The joy, it turns out, is in the trying.

I will always hear Bill's voice when I play. Most of the time, I still don't *get it right*, but when I do, I have him to thank. And the fact that I keep on trying—I have him to thank for that, too. I'm still waiting for the nod of approval that I never got in his studio, but now I realize the only nod I'll ever get will come from myself. Fly or fall. I get to choose. Maybe that's the most important thing he taught me. If I keep trying, I'm bound to fly.

"There was an open casket," said my father, who attended Bill's funeral. "And there he was, looking just like Bill, except, you know, dead. But in his right hand was a set of pencils."

"No! Really? In the casket? The red and blue pencils?"

"And a green one, too."

"*Green?*" I said. "There was a green pencil, too? I never ever saw the green pencil. What did you have to do wrong to get the green pencil?"

"Well," said Dad. "Maybe you weren't as bad as you thought."

The Tattooed Bride

Today is my daughter's birthday. Julia was born thirteen years ago at a small hospital in a tiny town called Sieglar. John joined us in the delivery room for the C-section. The surgical scrubs they handed him were way too short and way too big, so he had to spend the entire procedure holding his pants up—not a bad thing, really, because what else is there for an expectant father to do? He clutched his pants with one hand, stroked my arm with the other, and watched as the doctor lifted Julia into the world. The umbilical cord was wrapped around her neck. She didn't cry at first, but after the doctor untangled her, she let out a refined yelp, then cooperated with the medical staff as they whisked her to the nursery. I missed those first few moments of her life, because I was busy getting stitched back together.

We have celebrated Julia's birthday with balloon parties and fairy parties, swim parties and pony parties, picnics and playgrounds and movies and lunch. One year, when her father was in charge, a magician with a sparkly red vest and a top hat showed up and performed Truly Amazing Card Tricks. But this year, too old for a kid's party and too young to invite boys, she has decided not to celebrate with her friends.

John is playing a big concert at the Philharmonie tonight, and I'll be playing the piano at a wedding not far from home. The happy couple booked me six months ago, and, even though the date fell on Julia's birthday, I accepted the job. We have fancy plans for our children this summer, and we welcome the extra cash.

I've been feeling stupid ever since. Now Julia is home by herself, doing homework and eating the dinner I prepared for her. She'll watch a little TV, practice the piano, and read. I head out the door and tell myself she's fine. It's June, it's wedding season, I have a job to do. I'll bake a cake tomorrow.

⁐

The rain stops. I jump out of my car and my feet skid in the mud. The hem of my chiffon gown catches in the heel of my sandal. I bought these shoes at Bergdorf Goodman twenty years ago. They've held up quite nicely, through dozens of Manhattan chase-the-taxi dashes and decades of marble hotel floors, but they weren't designed to handle last-minute scurries through swamps in the German countryside. I regain my balance by grabbing the side of a snappy silver Mercedes sedan—not mine—wipe the goop off of my shoes with a couple of dead leaves, and do the little-old-lady-don't-wanna-fall walk through the parking lot.

I've heard about this place, but I've never played the piano here. It's not my regular castle, but a lesser castle, situated in a small forest ten minutes from where I live. It's five minutes before six, and I'm scheduled to play for a wedding dinner at six sharp. I've never figured out why it's so difficult to be punctual for a gig that's this close to home, but that's the way it goes.

It starts to sprinkle again just as I reach the cobblestone sidewalk, which turns out to be even more hazardous than the muck.

Slippery cobblestones + Stilettos = Blond on her butt.

At last I see the castle looming in the mist, in exactly the way a castle is supposed to loom. I've been in Germany for fourteen years, and I still thrill to the sight of these old chateaus. We didn't have any castles in Pittsburgh.

But something is amiss. This castle is kind of funky. For one thing, it's pink. I have a moment of Brothers Grimm—induced panic, but I snap out of it when my heel sticks between a couple of stones and I'm almost catapulted into a patch of stinging nettle. I recover, smooth my rain-ruined hair, and proceed. Clusters of casually dressed people lounge in the front garden. They're wearing T-shirts, shorts, and synthetic-fiber sundresses in peculiar shades of green and orange, and they're draped over benches and tables and each other, almost as if they're sleeping. It looks a little like a Jim Jones purple Kool-Aid kind of scene, but I hear one or two of them snort, so I know they are not dead.

Must be another party. A lot of these castle places are like American banquet halls, capable of hosting several celebrations at once. But these folks, slumped and silent, don't look like they're celebrating anything. I sneak past them—why don't they go inside to get out of the rain?—and hear someone snicker. I glance over my shoulder and catch a couple of scary-looking guys with shaved heads staring at me. Maybe skinheads, maybe not. So many men are shaving their heads these days.

Okay. Find the piano.

I'm greeted by an elegant man in a tuxedo. He has a full head of hair and he's handsome, James Bond–ish in the Sean Connery way, minus the height and the martini glass.

"Good evening, Frau Goldsby," he says.

"You must be Herr Dinkeldein," I say.

"Yes! So nice of you to be with us tonight. Our guests are out-side enjoying the fresh air. The bride has been kidnapped in the woods—it's some sort of Bavarian game the bride's family insisted on playing. Her kidnappers should return her soon."

"What fun!" I say. And I thought American Catholic weddings were weird.

"I'm so hoping you'll play the Pachelbel Canon in D for us, before we start dinner. I heard it on one of your CDs, and I adore that piece."

"What a lovely choice," I say. "I'll be glad to play it." I am up to my eyeballs in Pachelbel this season. Every bridal party wants it, and every bridal party thinks they are the first to request it.

"I will gather everyone for dinner, and once they are seated, I will introduce you. After the Pachelbel the buffet will open, and I'd like you to switch to background music at that point."

"That's a great idea." I glance at the piano. This handsome man in the expensive suit has rented a Bösendorfer concert grand for me. It's a 100,000-dollar instrument, and, for tonight, it's all mine. My goodness.

I wonder if I have time to call Julia before I start playing.

"The technician was here this afternoon. The piano is in good shape."

"Wonderful," I say. "I can't remember the last time—"

A shriek from the garden cuts off the rest of my sentence.

"There's my wife!" says Herr Dinkeldein.

I look out the front door and there she is, indeed. The blushing bride, Frau Dinkeldein—all 300 pounds of her—is galloping down the cobblestone path toward the pink castle, chased by a gaggle of tuxedo-clad men with shaved heads. She is moving at an amazing speed for someone her size. Obviously she is not wearing stilettos. But she is wearing a whiter-than-white strapless full-length dress, which she has hiked up around her, uh, substantial thighs.

"Wow," I say. "Wow."

"Isn't she something?" says Herr Dinkeldein. He is beaming. We stand shoulder to shoulder, nodding at Frau Dinkeldein, who truly resembles a charging bull in a Vera Wang plus-sized evening gown.

"I guess the kidnappers didn't nab her," I say.

"Oh," he says. "She's way too much woman for those guys to catch."

I'll say.

The lounging people in the park, the ones dressed in orange and green, begin to cheer. Oh no, it can't be. But yes, they are the guests. The corpulent bride and the shrunken James Bond groom have invited a bunch of German rednecks to their wedding. I'm missing my daughter's thirteenth birthday for this.

"I'll call everyone to dinner," says Herr Dinkeldein.

"I'll check the piano," I say. The piano is perfect. Exquisite, in fact. I retreat to the foyer and wait to be introduced. I try to call home but there's no cell-phone connection. The castle walls are way too thick.

The guests plop into their chairs. They look exhausted.

"We are honored to have Frau Goldsby with us tonight," says Herr Dinkeldein. He continues with his introduction, and I take in the small crowd gathered for the nuptial dinner. There are about six large round tables, each one holding eight guests. The skinheads and their dates are to my right. The dates have big hair, big boobs, and piercings in places that make me squirm. The men have tattoos and no hair.

So. Pachelbel it is. As I play the opening chords I look to the table on my left. It's very close to the piano, and I notice that several of the guests seated there—no, all of them—have a wart problem. What's with that?

Skinheads on the right. The Wart People on the left. I close my eyes and play. This piano is a dream come true, so I enter Pianoland and focus on the music. I call it the Pachelbel moment. It doesn't always happen, but when it does, it's magic. People love this piece of music, and I admit I love playing it. For a musician this is like confessing to a Twinkie addiction, but what can I say? In spite of my rolled eyes and tortured *not that piece again* proclamations, I dig playing it. It's neither difficult nor boring, categories into which most pieces of music fall. I can tart it up or dress it down, play it long or short, big or small (I like small), and still everyone recognizes it. When they hear the Canon in D they do that little smiling-nodding thing that makes me feel validated.

As I start the familiar sixteenth-note section of the melody I open my eyes. No one smiles and no one nods. One of the skinheads cracks his knuckles. And then, the mother of the bride gets up to dance. With her dog. I keep playing.

The dog is not one of those little Paris Hilton rat dogs. He is a midsized dog with floppy ears and a serious under-bite, and he probably weighs a good fifty pounds. The groom's mother, who is wearing a green sequined frock, holds Fido tightly and sways back and forth. Everyone ignores her. But to me, this is something special. I once had a singing dog (at the better castle) who howled whenever I played selections from *Phantom of the Opera*, but a dancing dog? This is a first.

George Romero would have a field day with this crowd: *Night of the Living Wedding*. The zombie guests stare into space as I begin improvising.

The bride's back is to me, and because of the strapless dress and the chair, she looks like she's naked. Why oh why would anyone with biceps that size wear a strapless dress? Maybe she couldn't find sleeves that fit. An intricate tattoo of a butterfly adorns most of her right shoulder and upper back. The artwork is remarkable, but it panics me to look at the tattoo. If I stare at it long enough I feel like I'm trapped inside a kaleidoscope.

Focus on the music.

This piano sings! What an instrument. The notes are like jewels, or stars, or any fine thing that glitters.

I look up. The paint on the ceiling is cracked and peeling, and I notice the crystal chandelier is covered with dust and missing a few pieces. More than a few. This place is run down—charming but seedy. I play the last chord of the Canon and let it ring.

Considering the comatose state of everyone except the woman dancing with the dog, I'm not expecting much applause, but one of the skinheads stands up and yells YEOW!!!!! and makes a hooting sound while pumping his fist. All of the skinheads pound on the table with their silverware. The groom stands to make another speech.

"I am moved to tears by this music," he says. "And now, dinner is served." All fifty guests, led by the Wart People, rush to the buffet. The bride makes a beeline for the piano. I've never seen someone so large move so quickly, except maybe in a Pittsburgh Steelers game. Franco Harris comes to mind.

"*FABELHAFT!!!*" she yells at me. She has buck teeth with wide spaces between them. I remember one of my dad's jokes about a girl eating an apple through a picket fence. She slaps me on the back and says, "*Sie sind echt cooooool!*" Another back slap.

It's like the German version of *Hee Haw* in this place.

One of the skinheads, the knuckle cracker, approaches the piano. "Can you play something by the Backstreet Boys?" he asks. I'm reminded of Jimmy Ciongoli, a pianist friend of my mine, who—when asked to play a Black Sabbath song—looked the customer right in the eye and said, "What the fuck's wrong with you?"

I want to say this, but I am poofy and polite and wearing 200-dollar golden sandals and a silk dress. So I smile and say, "I'm terribly sorry, but I don't know any Backstreet Boys music."

I knew the Backstreet Boys had a wide-reaching group of fans, but I had no idea they were popular with the tattooed skinhead crowd.

Crack, crack, crack. He glares at me and tugs at his orange T-shirt.

"Those are wonderful tattoos," I say. "Just wonderful."

Crack.

"Fresh ink," he says. "Got them for the wedding."

"Very, very nice," I say. "Lovely! Look at that. I've never seen a tattoo of a wild boar!"

Crack, crack.

There are two types of people in this world: those who run away from needles, and those who crave them. He smiles sadly, like he feels sorry for me, and walks away. I can hear his knuckles from all the way across the room.

I put on my *don't bother me I'm an artist* face and try to get back to that place where nothing counts but the music, but I'm interrupted by a Wart Person who wants to sing; I'm interrupted by the bride's mother, who wants to know if her dog can sleep under the piano; I'm interrupted by the handsome groom, who drinks too much and cries when he talks to me; I'm interrupted by the image of my daughter practicing the piano so she can grow up and someday play a job just like this one.

I play and play, until the guests have eaten themselves into a collective chocolate-truffle-induced coma. The room grows quiet, except for the occasional hoot of laughter coming from the bride's table, the cracking knuckles, and the gentle snoring of the dog at my feet. There are no wrong notes on this piano, no shadows or sharp corners, only sparkling light and the curved edges of the instrument's well-worn tones. I play a Debussy Arabesque, fully aware that I'm playing well, and equally aware that no one is conscious enough to care.

I glance through the French doors leading into the overgrown rose garden and see the muted colors of an early summer evening— soft pinks and lavenders, a garden's version of a sunset. I see the history of the castle in the rough stone walls surrounding the property, the majestic red maple trees towering over the crumbling gatehouse. And then I see the bride's brother barfing in the bushes.

So much for the Debussy. I keep playing, but I've lost my groove. I don't want to look at the barfing man, but I can't stop myself from staring. No one in the dining room can see him, but the piano is angled so that I have a perfect view of the action.

I'm not a snob; really I'm not. I have played for the great unwashed plenty of times and have truly enjoyed myself. But the barfing man pushes me a step too far. I am confused by this event. The classy (and weeping) groom, the *Hee Haw* bride; kidnappings and green and orange outfits; skinheads and people with warts; the mother of the bride with a dancing dog; and a member of the wedding party performing the Technicolor yawn right there in the garden.

I feel a tap on my shoulder. "*Guten Abend*, Frau Goldsby. As soon as you finish, I'll start my part of the program."

"Oh," I say. "Fine. What do you do?"

"I'm a magician," he says. "I do Truly Amazing Card Tricks." His red vest looks familiar. I think he's the same guy who worked at Julia's birthday party a couple of years ago. The dog starts to growl from under the piano.

"*Wunderbar!*" I say, playing my final chord. "That's it for me. Have a great evening! But one word of advice."

"Yes?"

"Whatever you do, *whatever you do*, don't look at the man crouching in the rose garden."

"Where?"

"Out there." I point.

Of course, he looks, just as the barfing man heaves one last time.

"*Mein Gott*," he says.

I say a silent goodbye to the magnificent Bösendorfer, collect the envelope of cash left for me in the caterer's office, and step into the June twilight. The rain has stopped and the air smells green and silvery.

Other than making a living, I wonder what I'm doing with my life. Making music?

Oh. That.

And missing Julia's birthday, I'm doing that, too. A country-western songwriter could write a decent "Delta Dawn" kind of lyric about this. But I'm not a country-western songwriter; I'm just a mom who works, maybe a little too much. My kids are growing up. They'll be flying away from me this summer, to the USA, to Sicily, to South Africa. I've played this gig tonight to help finance their adventures. In a few years they'll be gone for good. Then I'll play jobs like this to finance our reunions. Maybe we should all just stay home.

From the parking lot I hear the thump of a Backstreet Boys bass line. The puddles have evaporated. I hurry to my car, wondering how many centuries of magic and music this castle has endured, and how much of it cast a spell worth remembering.

The Piano Tuner

It's March, and icy rain stings my face, seeps under my collar, and soaks through my woolen socks. I'm on a walking tour of Vilnius, Lithuania, trying unsuccessfully to convince myself that cold is a state of mind. Our tour guide, a lovely young woman named Ilona, tells us—in perfect English—about the marvels of Lithuanian architecture and the history of the city, but I'm so cold I can't concentrate. Ilona doesn't seem the least bit chilly. Obviously her boots are better insulated than mine. Or maybe she's used to the climate. I huddle curbside with my American pals Julie and Tricia and hope for the tour to end soon.

"We are so lucky to get to see this beautiful city," says Tricia, pulling her hat low over her eyes.

"So lucky. We really are. So, so lucky," says Julie. She is struggling to send a text message and photo to her daughters without getting her iPhone wet.

I'm in town to perform for the Federation of American Women's Clubs Overseas—a wonderful international organization with the unfortunate acronym FAWCO. Say the name FAWCO after two glasses of wine and you're likely to raise a few eyebrows.

Along with two dozen other FAWCO delegates from places like Dubai, Marrakech, Paris, and Copenhagen, I have spent the morning looking at very old Lithuanian churches. A recently designated UNESCO World Heritage Site, Vilnius is home to some splendid architecture. This is all very nice, but right now I'm worried about my fingers. They feel like narrow slabs of marble. Goethe called architecture "frozen music." Frozen music will be on tonight's program if I don't get inside soon. I move closer to Tricia, who is seven months pregnant, hoping the heat radiating from her belly might keep me warm. Julie does the same thing. But even Tricia is freezing. We move in step, a synchronized pod on a frigid sightseeing excursion, and end up outside St. Anne's church, one of the architectural highlights of the Vilnius tour.

"Wow," says Julie, her teeth chattering. "That's *some* b-b-bell tower."

"This church," says Ilona, flinging one ungloved hand to the side, "is an example of both the 'flamboyant gothic' and 'brick gothic' styles of architecture."

"It looks more brickish than flamboyant to me," I say.

"Now we will end the regular part of the tour," says Ilona. "But for those of you hoping to see more, I will be glad to continue the tour inside the church."

"Do they have a fireplace in there?" I ask.

"No!" says Ilona. "That would be far too dangerous for the church."

"You know," says Julie, pointing to Tricia, who has been rendered speechless by the cold. "We have to get our p-p-pregnant friend some food. If we hurry we can get back to the hotel for the root-vegetable lunch. We just love the root vegetables served in your c-c-country."

Julie is my hero.

We shout goodbye and thank you, give Ilona a tip, perform a choreographed spin on our numbed-out heels, and rush to the nearest coffee shop—a fake Starbuck's with plush chairs and pleasant employees. I find a radiator, sit on it, and tuck my hands under my thighs. At times like this I feel very American.

Aside from warming up and eating a couple of turnips with gravy, I want to get back to the hotel to make sure the piano technician has arrived. I'm scheduled to play in five hours, and, even though I've requested a Steinway grand, the cash-strapped convention organizers have rented an upright that looks and sounds as if it's from another century. For all I know they borrowed it from the St. Anne's rectory. If the technician doesn't work some modern magic, I may have to pitch a fit and refuse to play. I've never done this in my life, but—in spite of my show-must-go-on nature—I'm not about to play for a sophisticated crowd of expatriate Americans and Lithuanian diplomats on a Crimean War–surplus clunker.

Tricia and Julie stay in the café, but I hurry back to the hotel, hoping to talk to the technician. On the way there I pass a strip club called GIRLS! GIRLS! GIRL! I do a double take on the missing "s" and wonder about the GIRL! Maybe she does the late shift all by herself. Or maybe she has the breakfast gig. I hope she has a warm outfit. The irony of an international women's conference taking place across the street from a lap-dancing parlor doesn't escape me.

In the hotel lobby I stop at the front desk to check for messages from the piano technician. Nothing. Now what? I'm not in the mood for more carrots and potatoes. Maybe I should have a cup of tea and come up with a plan. At least my hands are thawing. I've got a feeling the technician will be a no-show.

There's a nice Yamaha grand here in the lobby bar, but management has refused to move it to the ballroom for tonight's event. I would sit down and wait for the technician, but large men in leather jackets are taking up every seat in the lounge. Gold-toothed and sullen, they guzzle shots of vodka and look as if they're waiting for some sort of action. Perhaps they got lost on their way to GIRLS! GIRLS! GIRL! Or maybe they heard someone say FAWCO the wrong way and thought they might get lucky. I'm quite sure they're not here for the root-vegetable lunch special or the seminar on development grants.

Maybe the technician is upstairs in the ballroom. I wait ten minutes for an elevator that never arrives, then head to the staircase. The ballroom consumes most of the hotel's fourth floor. It's vast—way too much space for solo piano—and the instrument looks pathetic on the massive stage.

I greet the soundman just as a boy carrying an old-fashioned metal lunch box enters the room. He's twelve, fourteen at the most. He exchanges a few Lithuanian words with the soundman. His voice hasn't changed.

"Here is tuner," the soundman says to me. "Here is Viktorus."

The boy bows.

"*You're* the tuner?" I ask.

"I am Viktorus," he says. "I am tuner."

"He is tuner. He is Viktorus," says the soundman. "He come from school."

I am doomed. I have the world's most out-of-tune piano, made by a company that spells its name with letters not existing in Western alphabets, and a seventh-grade boy for a technician. I'm tempted to cancel the gig right now, but I don't want to hurt Viktorus's feelings. I have a son the same age, and this sweet-faced kid with the stained cardigan breaks my heart. I wonder if there are child-labor laws for piano tuners. I shake his hand and wish him luck.

"I go work," he says.

"This is a very bad piano," I say. He tilts his head and narrows his eyes, and I get the feeling he doesn't understand me. I don't speak Lithuanian, and I know the Lithuanians don't want to hear German, so I resort to speaking caveman English. "Piano very bad," I say, speaking loudly and slowly. I play a few notes and hold my ears. "No good piano. Very bad piano."

"Yes," he says. "Very bad piano."

"No worry," says the soundman. "Viktorus is Number One."

"I'll leave you alone to work," I say. "Do you want something to eat? A glass of milk?" I've offered a lot of beverages to piano technicians over the years, but milk isn't one of them.

The soundman translates for me.

"Thank you, no," Viktorus says, with another little bow. "My mother, she make dinner." He taps his lunch pail. I wonder if he has turnips in there.

"When should I come back?" I ask, pointing at my watch. "When?"

"Two hours," says Viktorus. "Very bad piano take very long time." And with that he pulls a tuning fork out of his lunch pail and sits down on the bench.

"Goodbye," I say.

"Goodbye-bye," says Viktorus.

I hike up another four flights of stairs to my room. I'm thirsty. There's no water in my minibar fridge. Instead, there are exactly fourteen tiny bottles of vodka.   I am tempted.

∽

Last night I was invited to a traditional Lithuanian dinner. I'm a vegetarian, so I had the root-vegetable platter, a delicious combination of potatoes, rutabagas, and carrots smothered in a dairy-laden sauce, which, being a backsliding vegan, I truly enjoyed. Everyone else had the same thing, but with a hunk of meat on the side. The wine was excellent. After dinner a local dance troupe performed. The group featured a couple of pretty tambourine-toting women with hair coiled in braids on top of their heads, an older gentleman who stomped around and played an instrument that resembled an alpenhorn, and an assortment of strapping young men who forced us to pound on the tables and yell something that sounded like *hoopa shoopa shoy yoy yoy.* We tried to clap along with the odd-meter music, but—because of the wine—we were having trouble finding two and four, let alone five and nine.

The dancers' nineteenth-century Lithuanian peasant costumes, in vibrant blues, reds, greens, and yellows, drew a stark contrast to our little black dresses and dark pantsuits. Some of the Lithuanian men pulled American women up to dance—I was one of them— and we ended up in the show, doing a joyous Lithuanian folk dance called *rateliai.* I had a hard time keeping up with the spinning, but I liked shouting *hoopa!* whenever the head stomper pointed at me.

∽

Two hours have passed. I put on my gown and head back to the ballroom at five in the afternoon. I do not have a good feeling. I'm conflicted. Should I refuse to play and look like a jerk? Or should I play the rotten piano and have everyone think I'm a rotten pianist? Twenty years ago I would have played. Now I'm leaning toward exercising the diva option. But first I need to deal with Viktorus.

Waiters scurry from table to table, checking place settings and counting chairs. Viktorus is still at the piano making adjustments, his diminutive body bent over the strings.

"Hello, Viktorus!" I say. "Piano is good?"

"Piano is good," he says. "You play."

I sit on the bench and hold my breath before striking the first chord. It sounds beautiful. With cautious optimism I play through the entire range of the instrument. The piano sounds and feels as good as any small piano can sound. Viktorus is a twelve-year-old magician. I have no idea how he has coaxed the once-hopeless pile of junk into such great shape, but I yell *hoopa!* Then I jump up and shake his fragile hand.

"Thank you," I say. "Thank you."

"Please," says Viktorus. "Please."

He packs his tools into his lunch pail, smiles at me, and heads into the kitchen.

An hour later around 250 FAWCO members, the American ambassador to Lithuania, the Lithuanian undersecretary of state, and a handful of other dignitaries arrive. I'm scheduled to start the program with the Lithuanian national anthem, which, truth be told, is a nice tune. My husband has added some jazzy chord changes. He knows I'm uneasy about causing an international incident, so he has exercised some restraint with the flatted ninths. I've suggested passing out song sheets so the Americans can sing along, but there's hardly a word in the text that any of us would be able to pronounce—way too many consonants and upside-down triangles. It won't be a sing-along kind of evening.

"Ladies and gentlemen, please stand for the Lithuanian national anthem."

Here we go. I sit at Viktorus's scratched, chipped, and beautifully tuned piano and play the introduction. The soundman has the piano hyper-miked, giving the little instrument an enormous presence. The Lithuanian delegation places their hands over their hearts, and the Americans follow suit. Halfway through the first verse I realize what I'm playing sounds suspiciously like a Cole Porter ballad. The Lithuanian VIPs at the head table sing and wipe away tears. Good sign or bad, I'm not sure.

By the time I start the second verse, I've drifted into a national anthem reverie. How long has it been since I've stood at attention for the "Star-Spangled Banner"? Do I even remember the words? Of course I do.

I play the last chord and it rings out, in tune and clear. There's thunderous applause, not for my performance, but for Lithuania and this moment of national pride. Everyone sits down. I look out at the crowd. Across the ballroom, in a white shirt and tie, is Viktorus, He has saved the day. I know it. He knows it. No frozen music tonight. The show will go on.

I wave to Viktorus and blow a kiss. He bows, puts on a jacket, and dashes out of sight, an adolescent boy with a tuning fork and a lunch pail, finding his way in the midwinter Vilnius rain.

Piano Girl Medical
Emergency Redux

I'm at the Studio Bühne Siegburg, a black-box theater not far from home. Located between Bonn and Cologne, Siegburg is a contemporary shopping town with a dozen hair salons, a dose of medieval flair, and just enough culture. In Germany even the smallest towns have funds allotted to the arts, a real advantage for freelance musicians and audiences alike. Tonight, together with performing artist Peggy O, I'll be presenting an English-German reading and concert featuring selections from *Piano Girl*, my memoir of working the cocktail-lounge circuit. *Piano Girl Live* is a fun program, and I'm looking forward to tonight's performance.

Due to the popularity of Siegburg resident Peggy O, the event has been sold out for two weeks. *Piano Girl Live* has been advertised as a two-language performance, and we're expecting a hip crowd, or at least a multilingual crowd. I'll present some of the chapters in English, and Peggy O will cover the German part of the evening. While she's reading my stories I'll provide a piano score for her performance.

It's late November—right in the middle of my busy season—and we haven't had much rehearsal time. But I'm not concerned. Peggy and I have worked together before, there's a cool technician named Ulli running lights and sound, and a decent Bechstein grand piano. Barring disaster, we've got an easy night ahead of us.

I've planned a two-hour show, including intermission. The first half goes smoothly—the piano is almost in tune, my fingers are working, and the English-as-a-second-language audience laughs when they're supposed to. People watching a program in a foreign language always seem to laugh louder, maybe because they're grateful to understand the humor. The joy of tonight's German audience charms me—I know how hard they're working to get the jokes.

At the break Peg and I meet in the dressing room—a freezing basement storage area littered with old props and bits of decaying feather boas—and share one cracked mirror to touch up our makeup for the second half. Peggy O, a gymnast turned cabaret performer, is tiny and muscular, with pixie-cut black hair and an elfin grin. She's the physical opposite of me, which may be why we work well together. She reapplies her lipstick and sits on the floor to stretch. She's always stretching. Maybe I should do more of that. I watch as she puts one leg over her head, and then the other.

"Good crowd," she says.

"Yes! And you sound wonderful," I say.

"Really? I thought I flubbed that second text."

"If you did I didn't hear it."

"Are you sure?"

"I'm sure. Do I look fat?"

"No."

Ulli, who also functions as the stage manager and caterer, comes downstairs to fetch us. I'm looking forward to getting back onstage, just to get warm. I hope my fingers aren't stiff.

"Ready?" I say to Peggy. She untwists her limbs and jumps to her feet.

"*Ja! Los geht's.*"

To start the second half I play a medley of my own compositions. The piano is too bright in the upper register and too muddy
in the middle, but I'll live.

Next up, Peg reads a piece called "Playback 1979," the true
story of a choking priest who collapsed while I was performing
at the Redwood Motor Inn on Banksville Road in Pittsburgh, a
venue known for buffalo wings, crab cakes, popcorn shrimp, and
supercharged extra-shot-for-a-dollar cocktails. Cheers. In the story,
which Peggy O reads with great zeal, a group of priests shows up
for the Friday-night happy hour. I play "Amazing Grace," my one
religious number, and two people get up to dance. The food-and-
beverage manager yells at me for playing too loudly. While he's
reprimanding me, one of the priests, a guy named Father Louie,
eats a crab cake and starts to choke. He makes horrible noises and
then collapses. The room manager tells me to play louder so the
guests don't notice the choking priest. The priest is flat on the floor,
and I'm banging out "I Feel the Earth Move."

The choking-priest incident wasn't one of my finer artistic
moments, but I was twenty years old and lacking finesse. In retro-
spect it's a funny story, one that can be told cheerfully and without
sorrow, but one that has needed a couple of decades to ferment for
me to appreciate it.

So. Here we are in the middle of the episode, with Peggy acting it out in German while I plod through "Amazing Grace"—part
of the tale's musical landscape. A *rumple rumple* noise comes out of
the audience, stage left.

Rumple rumple. There it is again.

Peggy O is not getting the laughs she usually gets while reading this section. Something is up.

Rumple rumple.

Shit.

Peggy O reads the lines, "He's choking, he's choking, he's choking. Heart attack, heart attack, heart attack! Someone call a doctor! We need a doctor! We need a doctor!"

Rumple rumple.

"I have to stop!" she says, throwing down her text. She shields her eyes from the spotlight as she peers into the audience, trying to figure out the source of the rumple. I puff out my cheeks like a blowfish—a bad habit of mine when I'm nervous—and keep playing "Amazing Grace." I feel disconnected, as if I've been zapped back to the Redwood Motor Inn.

"Excuse me!" Peggy O says. "There's a big *rumple rumple* out there. Is everything okay? It almost sounds like the story I'm reading—like someone out there needs a doctor."

We hear a gasp, a shout, then the sound of an audience member falling to the floor. Rumple rumple, indeed.

A voice from the audience calls out, "We need a doctor!"

Peggy O says, *"Really?"*

"Call a doctor! Call a doctor!"

I'm just getting ready to start the vamp to "I Feel the Earth Move."

The house lights come up and Ulli hustles over to the fallen woman. I wait for someone to tell me what to do, but then realize it's my show and I'm in charge. So I do what any self-respecting musician would do under similar circumstances. I take a break.

My husband meets me in the wings and pushes me back onstage with instructions to *say something*.

"Ladies and gentlemen, we'll be taking a short intermission for, uh, obvious reasons. Stick around, we'll be right back." I'm thinking of mentioning the books and CDs for sale in the lobby, but the paramedics burst into the theater. I've been upstaged.

I return to the wings and wait with my husband, Peggy O, and Ulli. We make small talk while the paramedics do their thing.

"Poor woman!" says Peggy O. "It's so stuffy—no wonder she fainted. You need an air conditioner in here."

"We're lucky we have a piano and lights," says Ulli.

"Maybe we should take a collection," says Peggy O. I detect a note of sarcasm.

"Did anyone catch her when she fainted?" I ask.

"No idea," says the stage manager. "I would have turned the lights up sooner, but I thought she was part of the show."

The paramedics transport the unfortunate woman from the third row of the Studio Bühne to the hospital, conveniently located next door. The Siegburg city planners have thought of everything. They carry her right out the stage door and up the ramp to the emergency room.

Like most musicians, I'm no stranger to weird events, but the timing of this particular medical emergency—right in the middle of a medical-emergency story—astounds me. It's almost like the woman got the idea to collapse from listening to the reading.

We need a doctor!

No, we need a doctor!

No, we need a doctor!

I guess everyone needs a doctor at some point. Oh, the power of suggestion. Good thing we didn't present the story about the two customers having sex in the middle of the Manhattan Grand Hyatt cocktail lounge. We might have had a full-fledged orgy break out stage left.

After a ten-minute intermission, my husband suggests I return to the stage.

"What do I do?" I ask.

"*Say something*," he says. "And then sit down and play."

"Ladies and gentlemen, due to the, uh, medical emergency, we won't be continuing with the choking-priest story. You'll have to read *Piano Girl* to see how that particular emergency turns out. Books are for sale in the lobby. Thank you for your patience. I've been assured by the paramedics that our friend from the third row will be fine."

I have no idea if this is true, but I'm an optimist, and I figure if we're going to make it through the rest of the performance, the audience shouldn't be thinking that Madame might be expiring next door in the *Krankenhaus*. I play an uplifting piano solo in a major key to lead us into the next part of the show, called "Here Comes That Bride." No one faints or chokes or collapses in that story so I figure we're safe. We bounce back and so does the audience. They're generous with their applause. Evening over.

After the show I stand on one side of the lobby, sip a glass of wine, and sign books and CDs. A *Piano Girl* fan asks if the fallen woman purchased a CD during intermission.

"*Why?*" I ask. "Exactly what do you mean by that?" I'm a little sensitive about these things. My music—which tends to be floaty—has become popular in hospitals and rehab clinics. In the past year I've had several people tell me their relatives passed away while listening to my recordings. Just last month my mother was in a funeral home in Pittsburgh, and they had my CD on the playlist.

"Just thought she might want something to listen to while she's recovering," says the fan.

Later in the evening, Peggy O calls to tell me the unfortunate woman—like the choking priest—has survived, she's feeling much better, and she'll be released from the hospital in the morning. Peggy O assures me the heat, not the music, caused her to lose consciousness.

"By the way," Peggy O says. "She loved the show."

The Vision

I liked the Greek Guys. If you were one of the 125 million people who tuned in to the 2010 *Eurovision Song Contest*, broadcast live from Oslo, Norway, you know what I'm talking about. The Greek Guys wore tight white jumpsuits and dangerous-looking black leather boots, and stomped all over the stage yelling *"Opa!"* while life-threatening flames shot up behind them. Bring on the octopus! Break a plate! The song itself was nothing more than an odd-meter Greek hootenanny with machine-gun electronic percussion, and the lead singer was more of a lead shouter, but in the hot-blooded macho entertainment category, the Greek Guys hit a home run.

Acres of crushed velvet! Singers with figure skaters! Strippers and cellists and cleavage and lace! With a bigger audience than the Super Bowl, *Eurovision* is the only television event where a tenor can attract a larger crowd than a quarterback. It's music as sport, even though music has little to do with the outcome. Most Americans don't know about *Eurovision*. The program depends on a break-free show—there are no commercials—while most American television depends on advertising. Sitting down to watch *Eurovision* is like jumping onto a three-hour roller-coaster ride, complete with loop-de-loops and breathtaking curves on the bumpy track. It's a nonstop one-night event broadcast to countries that belong to the

European Broadcasting Union, which, to the confusion of first-time viewers, includes places like Israel, Turkey, Russia, and Georgia.

"Moldova is the one to watch," said my pal Sharon Reamer, a geophysicist and a longtime *Eurovision* fan and expert. "They always get most everyone in the entire country onstage, including someone's great-grandmother wearing a babushka and a hand-embroidered costume." In a surprise twist, this year's Moldova entry didn't include a grandmother, but instead featured a hip-thrusting alto saxophone player in a blue sparkle Elvis jumpsuit, assisted by a Moldovan Lady Gaga clone and a man who resembled a pipe cleaner but sounded just like Tom Jones.

Dry ice! Half-naked dancers! Backup singers in orange Afro wigs!

Armenia's song, "Apricot Stone," took up the grandmother slack by plopping an eighty-year-old woman in the middle of an Armenian historical drama. A man wearing burlap knickers back-flipped over the grandmother. Not that anyone noticed. All eyes were on lead singer Eva Rivas's cleavage. Most male viewers, I'm sure, were wondering just where she was hiding that apricot stone. When I suggested it might be tangled in her hair extensions, my teenage son, who was watching with me, called me a poor sport and said I didn't grasp the message in her song.

I was drawn to Romania and their presentation of "Playing with Fire." In addition to their creative use of latex and a Las Vegas–inspired Plexiglas double keyboard, Paula Seling and Ovi actually knew how to sing. Paula Seling looked nasty, in a good way. Ovi did his best to keep up with her, but he could have used a few macho lessons from the Greek Guys. Or maybe he just needed a last name. Ovi Love, Ovi Ivo, or maybe Ovi da Rainbow.

Spain's entry, Daniel Diges singing "Algo Pequeñito," had a Fellini-meets-Cirque du Soleil vibe. The acrobatic clowns in Daniel's chorus line bordered on creepy with their chalky faces and waxy lips, but I liked Daniel's appearance a lot, especially his hair; he looked like Malcolm Gladwell in a severe windstorm, always a clever guise for anyone hoping to pull focus from a dozen dancing Bozo look-alikes.

Denmark turned in a performance right out of the eighties, a decade I particularly enjoyed the first time around. The two performers, Chanée and N'evergreen, couldn't decide if they wanted to pay tribute to Abba or the Police, so, in a move that impressed me with its inclusiveness, they did both, while wearing Captain and Tennille military jackets.

Every year one country or another adds a stripper to its *Eurovision* presentation, hoping to garner extra points for showing extra body parts. This time around, Turkey—in a clever nod to heavy-metal music—featured a stripping female robot, a ploy that might have worked in their favor if the robot's head had not gotten snagged on her breastplate early in the song. Georgia's Sopho Nizharadze belted out a high G while standing on her head, so she didn't need to strip. England's bump-and-grind action came from a Hugh Grant look-alike who bounced around the stage while performing something best described as Disco Duck does Donna Summer. He never took his clothes off, but he should have.

I loved them all.

Iceland showcased a woman with a voice so brassy it might have caused that volcanic eruption, Ireland presented a promising singer having a bad hair day, and Azerbaijan made a big splash with a Celine Dion–influenced "Drip Drop" song. France's entry? It was more like France's exit. Monsieur Matador's derrière was music for my eyes.

The show's viewers, armed with cell phones and copious amounts of sparkling wine, ouzo, and beer, help determine the winner every year. They gather in nightclubs, corner bars, gay bars, at public viewing screens in town centers, and in living rooms— like mine—with their families. They aren't permitted to vote for their own country's entry. In the past, *Eurovision* has been accused of being a contest for favored nations. Germany, not high on the popularity list, often finished close to the bottom. But a new system requires each country to provide a small jury of music-industry professionals to contribute fifty percent of the vote. That's made it easier for less popular nations to compete and win.

My very favorite performer was Belgian Tom Dice, who stood alone onstage with his guitar and sang a song about a man standing alone onstage with his guitar. I actually phoned the number and voted for him, because I'm a sucker for singer-songwriters. Then again, I'm fifty-three and still believe that music should be played by real musicians.

Germany's performer, the Lolita-inspired Lena, looked really cute in her Brit-suave black shift but danced like she was in need of a trip to the nearest Australian loo—her fake English accent had the unfortunate effect of making her sound like a shepherd from somewhere north of Melbourne. But Lena brought down the house. After all the votes were tallied, she won, which proves once and for all that you don't need a stripping robot if you're wearing the perfect little black dress. Lena was cool, and so was her song. Aside from one reference in the lyric to blue underwear, there was nothing too embarrassing about her performance.

Budding talent-show producers take note: *Eurovision* maintains its party vibe because it refuses to follow the *Star Search* formula. There are no critiques or mean-spirited comments from a jury of over-gelled celebrity has-beens, and the international voting remains secret, right up until the very end. No one leaves the stage humiliated. We don't see anyone go home in tears. At times, *Eurovision* seems like one of those kindergarten competitions where everyone gets a prize just for trying. And maybe that's the way it should be.

By the end of the 2010 *Eurovision* show, I had decided that all of the performances, even the ones using the most spandex, were about something bigger than the song, the singer, or the country. As the jury tabulated votes, the Norwegian producers of this year's show broadcast a live dancing segment. Tens of thousands of amateur dancers from all corners of Europe, who had learned a simple routine, waved their arms and kicked their legs in time to a silly techno anthem meant to unite us all. It worked. We witnessed a funky collage of real people making their own fun, and for a few glorious minutes in television land, we celebrated together. Most of us will never enter a talent show of this magnitude, but all of us— regardless of where we live—can laugh and sing along.

Meanwhile, each of the *Eurovision* performers, including the plain young man with the unadorned voice and simple guitar accompaniment, has gathered the courage to stand up in front of 125 million viewers and say, "Hey, this is who I am. This is where I come from. Hope you like it. But if not, that's okay."

Opa!

The Accidental Ambassadors

John, Curtis, and I stand in a clump next to a security gate at Cologne/Bonn International Airport. Curtis leaves today for an eight-week student-exchange trip to South Africa. He'll be flying alone, first to Amsterdam and then to Cape Town, where, hopefully, Chris Coetzee and his parents will be waiting for him. Curtis will live with the Coetzee family and attend a private high school called Somerset College, close to the Stellenbosch mountain range. The Coetzee family will take care of Curtis while he's there, and we'll do the same for Chris when he comes to Germany. A lot could go wrong with a plan like this, and I've got a case of maternal jitters.

The boys have gotten to know each other through Facebook. I've had plenty of e-mail contact with Renée, Chris's mother, and she seems efficient, kind, and concerned about the right things—warm clothes for Curtis, potential food allergies, getting to the airport on time to meet him. I tell myself that anyone who is worried about my son's insulated hiking boots and apple allergy is probably not an ax murderer planning to sell his limbs to Satan worshipers in Botswana. Or worse.

In his carry-on bag he has an iPod with volumes four through six of the Harry Potter audio series, half of a baguette smeared with butter, his passport, and 100 euros cash for an emergency. I have yet to encounter any real emergency that could be solved with 100 euros, but giving him more seems overindulgent.

Time to go. I hold it together when Curtis bends down to say goodbye, but just barely. *It's only eight weeks*, I tell myself. I stand on my toes so I can get my head into the spot between his shoulder and his neck. I close my eyes and inhale the mingled scents of cologne, deodorant, and boy.

Mothers have been sending their sons away from home since the beginning of time, for far more worrisome activities than an eight-week exchange program. It's ridiculous to be so emotional.

Curtis is a head taller than anyone else in the security line, so it's easy to watch from a distance as he navigates his way through the various stations. Every so often he sneaks a look over his shoulder to see if we're still there.

"I hope we're doing the right thing," says John. "I mean, we're sending him to Africa with a baguette and 100 euros."

Fourteen hours—that's how long it takes to fly from Germany to Cape Town, with a stop in Amsterdam to change planes. Sixteen years—that's how long it takes to raise a boy so he can leave home.

❧

Over the next eight weeks we hear just enough from Curtis. He sends occasional e-mails and calls us when we guilt him into it. We know that he's having fun at school, that he's participating in an African drumming workshop, and—much to his chagrin—learning to make African beaded jewelry. His sister finds the idea of Curtis at a craft table making earrings extremely funny. Renée sends me occasional updates and tells me how much she enjoys Curtis's company, how she loves listening to the boys tell stories and play the piano. Chris also plays alto and baritone saxophone, so there's a lot of music in the house.

Somerset College has organized a handful of exchange-student events, including a weeklong "survival" camping trip for the thirty international students who are currently visiting the school. Renée sends photos of Curtis and Chris—two happy boys at an elephant reserve, cautious boys petting a cheetah, somber boys on the boat to the infamous Robben Island, and joyful boys on the top edge of Table Mountain, looking as if they might leap into the abyss.

Curtis writes to us about seeing genuine poverty for the first time. He writes about long hikes, and the Stellenbosch wildflowers, and the way ostriches hang out roadside and baboons run wild. He writes about the view from the Cape of Good Hope, where the Atlantic and Indian oceans meet.

Later in the fall Chris arrives at Frankfurt International Airport to spend eight weeks with us. It's six in the morning, the plane is early, and we arrive on the other side of the Customs/Immigration area just as South African passengers begin to trickle through the sliding glass doors. I hate these doors. They never stay open long enough to determine who's on the other side.

"Do you see him?" I ask Curtis.

"Nope," he says. "Yes. Wait. No. Maybe."

The sliding doors close. It's freezing cold in the international-arrivals area. I'm holding hot chocolate and a large cinnamon pastry for Chris.

The doors slide open.

"There he is!" says Curtis.

"Where?" I say. I stand on my toes and the hot chocolate sloshes over my hand.

"There! I think I see his jacket."

The doors close. Open. Close. Open. Close.

Fifteen minutes later Chris emerges. He's a great-looking kid with dark hair, a crooked smile, and greenish-blue eyes. He and Curtis hug while I stand to the side and watch.

I dump the cold hot chocolate. We hurry to the car and head for home, with Curtis proudly pointing out the *Autobahn* sights along the way—no baboons or ostriches, but lots of well-maintained cars driving way too fast, indifferent sheep, grazing cows, and the occasional castle looming on a distant hill.

◌

Chris goes to school every day with Curtis and works on his German. His first language is Afrikaans, but most of his education has been in English. He also speaks a little Zulu, which doesn't get him very far in Germany. The boys travel to Berlin and stay in a youth hostel. I take them to Paris for a long weekend. They also accompany John to concerts and rehearsals.

Chris likes to hang out in a corner of our living room. He piles his books and laptop on an old end table, and sometimes his saxophone ends up there, too. He likes to play my piano, and he often practices while I'm cooking. Without being asked, Chris takes out the garbage, rakes the leaves, and sets the table while telling me stories about his country. He hopes to study medicine, become a doctor, and live and work in South Africa. Proud of the progress made there, he also acknowledges the need for further change. He's a young man with a boy's optimism.

MC Funk, Curtis's band, invites Chris to perform with them as a guest artist. One of their gigs, a four-hour, no-intermission community event called "Four Hundred Years of Klavier," stars a long-winded and pompous actor in a powdered wig. The wig man delivers coma-inducing speeches between pieces of music played by capable students from local schools. Different groups of musicians in unfortunate period costumes—including one nine-year-old Korean boy dressed as Beethoven—play beautifully. But the wig man drones on and on. By the time he introduces MC Funk, featuring Chris—the last act of the evening—the remaining audience members, glassy eyed and half dead from boredom, can hardly lift their hands to applaud. But the boys, buzzed from four hours of backstage cola and wearing their hip everyday clothes and retro sunglasses, coast onstage and, as Chris likes to say, "own it." They dig into a too-fast but groovy version of "Cantaloupe Island" and pull the audience back to consciousness. The wig man, rendered speechless by their teenage energy, picks at his embroidered waistcoat. I take pictures to send to Renée.

Everyone adores Chris. The girls think he's exotic because he comes from Africa, the boys think he's cool for the same reason. The adults, who don't really care where he comes from, like him because he's smart and polite.

One evening as I'm making dinner for Chris, Curtis, and David, our Iranian neighbor, I overhear the following conversation:

"It's so stupid to judge someone based on where he comes from," says David.

"True, that," says Chris. He likes to say *true, that.* It's a habit we've all started to pick up.

"Stereotypes are bad," says Curtis.

"True, that."

"When people find out I'm a white South African," says Chris, "they think I'm a racist."

"Yeah," says David. "When they find out I'm Iranian they think I'm a terrorist."

"Yeah," says Curtis. "When they discover I'm American they think I'm stupid."

"Why can't everyone just get along?"

"Right. We're all just people. And, really, we're pretty much the same."

"True, that."

❧

"Welcome to our Thanksgiving dinner!" says Volkmar Schultz, a seventy-two-year-old former politician and promoter of transatlantic cultural exchange. I'm attending tonight's dinner next door to the Cologne City Hall with Curtis, Chris, and Julia. Over 100 guests have been invited to share a traditional American meal with members of the Cologne-Indianapolis Friendship Circle.

I'm excited about this evening for a couple of reasons. I like Volkmar—he has attended a few of my concerts, and I've always enjoyed talking with him and his wife, Dorothea. Plus, I love Thanksgiving. I haven't had a traditional Thanksgiving dinner since the last time my parents visited me in Germany, ten years ago. My mom, the designated chef, had smuggled four cans of Libby's pumpkin-pie filling and three boxes of Pepperidge Farm stuffing croutons in her suitcase. Fearful she wouldn't be able to find a "normal" turkey in Germany, she tried to convince my father to pack a frozen twenty-pound bird, but he refused, not because he feared arrest at Customs, but because he couldn't find a suitcase in the right size.

I've convinced Curtis and Chris that this is the ultimate exchange-student experience—a South African teenager attending an American Thanksgiving dinner in Germany.

During the cocktail reception Julia stays by my side. Volkmar chats with the boys for a few minutes, introduces them to the American Consul General, the former mayor of Cologne, and some visiting dignitaries and students from Indianapolis. Then he circles around and returns to me.

"I'm so pleased you could come," he says.

"Thanks for including the kids," I say.

"Of course!" Volkmar says. "There's nothing like the exchange-student experience. Chris will carry his impressions of Germany back to South Africa. At the same time, he's making a lasting impression on your family and everyone who meets him. He's an ambassador!"

"Well, I don't know if he realizes that," I say. "Chris is busy being a teenager."

"Of course he doesn't know that now," says Volkmar. "But he'll find out later. These student exchanges create a closeness between people, and ultimately between nations. They're much more effective than politics in creating bonds, because they're built on people actually getting to know each other."

"Were you an exchange student, Volkmar?" I ask

"Yes," he says. He stops talking for a moment, then he smiles. "Yes, I was."

∽

In 1955, seventeen-year-old Volkmar Schultz traveled to America as an exchange student in a program sponsored by the US State Department. It was only ten years after the end of World War II, and America, along with much of the world, was still suspicious of Germany. The American Consul General told Volkmar to be a "good ambassador for the new Germany," to do more than just have fun. He should serve his host community, make a good impression, and promote German-American relations by being helpful, friendly, and cooperative. In other words, show the Americans that it was okay to like a German.

Volkmar, a lanky young man with a wide face and a smile to match, had a curious nature and an explorer's dreams. He sailed to the USA from Bremerhafen on a summer day. His mother, back home in Leverkusen, was convinced she would never see her son again. Uncle Fritz, the last person in the family to depart for the West, had left for Canada in 1929 and never returned. Certain Volkmar would follow Uncle Fritz's example, she refused to watch the ship carry her son away.

Several weeks later Volkmar arrived in Englewood, Ohio, a northern suburb of Dayton. He was met by Jim and Kathryn Lutz, a childless couple with a small home on Sweet Potato Ridge Road. They would be his American family for the next year. On Volkmar's first August night in Ohio, Mom Lutz served him homegrown corn on the cob. Like most Europeans, he had never seen a human being eat corn in this form. Anxious to live up to his role as an ambassador for the "new Germany," Volkmar attempted to cut into the cob with a knife and fork. After a proper demonstration from Pop, Volkmar slathered his corn with butter, picked up the cob with his hands, and tucked in.

Like most members of the Englewood community, Mom and Pop Lutz were salt-of-the-earth God-fearing members of the

Church of the Brethren. The Lutz social life revolved around church activities. Soon after Volkmar's arrival, Pop Lutz suggested that he go to the churchyard to help with the final phase of construction of the new church. Volkmar wasn't a religious boy, but, hoping to score points with Mom and Pop, he headed to the churchyard to pitch in. It was a sweltering Ohio summer day—a tough climate for a boy who had grown up in Germany. The construction boss sent Volkmar to the roof of the church—where it was even hotter—with instructions to begin nailing shingles. He spent much of the summer on the church roof in the intense sun, hammer in one hand, a bag of nails strapped over his shoulder, enthusiastically hammering one nail after another, finishing the roof on his adopted community's church.

Volkmar's German parents didn't own a telephone, so he wrote weekly letters to his mother, reporting on his life on Sweet Potato Ridge Road. He told her all about Mom Lutz—when she wasn't working at the Dayton employment office, she cooked and canned vegetables harvested from her back garden. She made fried chicken and blueberry and peach pies, baked beans and noodle soup—Ohio farm food.

Pop Lutz taught elementary school for nine months of the year. During the summer he made money painting houses, barns, and anything else that required a fresh coat of color or varnish. Volkmar earned seventy-five cents an hour painting for Pop—hard work in the heat and humidity. In the cooler night hours, Volkmar had a job chasing chickens for an Englewood farmer. He would head into the darkened barn with a few of his church friends, grab the birds, and stuff them into crates.

When he wasn't nailing shingles, chasing chickens, eating chickens, or splashing in the nearby Miller's Grove swimming pool, Volkmar hung out with the church youth group. He attended youth-group activities and Church of the Brethren weekday suppers and socials. He also helped plan the occasional Sunday service directed by youth-group members. During these services Volkmar stood before the congregation singing—with his German accent—selections from the Brethren Hymnal. Although the English lyrics were a challenge, the tunes were familiar. The Church of the Brethren had originated in Germany, and melodies from the hymnbook had traveled across the Atlantic with German settlers. Phyllis Warner, a young adult planning a career as a minister of music, accompanied Volkmar on the piano. Together they sang and played their way through a year of Sundays. Volkmar didn't always agree with the religious messages, but he figured music could help him fulfill his role as a good ambassador.

In spite of his mother's fear that he would never again set foot in Germany, Volkmar sailed back home one year after his departure. After attending universities in Cologne and Göttingen and spending another summer in Ohio with the Lutzes, he accepted a position as a public-relations officer for the city of Cologne. In 1980 he won election to the North Rhine Westphalia State Parliament, a position he held for fourteen years. When traveling to the USA for work, Volkmar often managed a visit to Sweet Potato Ridge Road. Over the decades he continued to exchange letters, phone calls, and visits with Mom and Pop Lutz. The Lutzes came to Germany several times, and Volkmar proudly showed them the progress made by the "new Germany."

Mom Lutz died in the autumn of 1989. Volkmar, who was at her side when she passed away, helped Pop and members of the church community bury his American mother in Bethel Cemetery, next to the church he had helped build. Several years later, Pop Lutz died and Volkmar again traveled to the graveyard next to the little church. It seemed the Englewood phase of his life was over.

In 1994 Volkmar was elected to the *Bundestag*—the German Senate. He focused on foreign relations and chose North America as his field of interest, traveling back and forth to Washington, discussing the reunification of Germany with State Department officials. Nearly forty years after his first unofficial assignment as an ambassador, Volkmar was at it again.

Whenever Volkmar visited the USA he stopped in Troy, Ohio, to visit Nancy Walker, a niece of Mom and Pop's who had settled there with her husband and children. In 2008, eager to show Englewood to Dorothea, his new wife, Volkmar toured the little town with her, pointing out the Lutz homestead and the church he had helped build. The visit culminated in a trip to the cemetery, where Volkmar and Dorothea stopped by the Lutz graves.

After a moment of silence they strolled through Bethel Cemetery, going row to row, carefully reading the granite markers, searching for names that Volkmar might recognize from 1955. It was a bleak September afternoon, the corn had been harvested, a cool wind blew through the barren fields surrounding the cemetery and swept dust and bits of old leaves around their feet. The sky, the color of pale cement, seemed cracked and fragile, as if pieces of clouds might break away and fall to the ground.

A pickup truck pulled into the graveyard and parked not far from where Volkmar and Dorothea stood. The passengers, an elderly woman and a youngish man, got out of the truck. They paused for a moment, looked at a tombstone, then began to approach.

The woman, in her seventies, with frothy white hair and a deep-blue woolen coat, waved at Volkmar and shouted, "May I help you with something? Are you looking for anyone in particular?"

"Not really," said Volkmar. "Just looking for names of people I used to know."

She came closer. Her eyes narrowed and the lines on her forehead deepened. The wind picked up.

"You are Volkmar," she said. "Volkmar Schultz."

"Yes," Volkmar said. "Yes, I am. How did you know?"

"I recognized your voice."

"My voice? I'm sorry, but I don't know who you are."

"I'm Phyllis Warner," she said. "I never forget a voice. I played the piano for you when you sang. You were the German boy. It was over fifty years ago, but the sound of your voice has stayed with me all these years. The sound of a voice is like a fingerprint—no two are alike. And your voice is especially unique."

Volkmar couldn't move. Over Phyllis's shoulder he saw the church steeple. He remembered what it felt like to be seventeen— uncertain and desperate to fit in, nailing shingles in the hot sun. He heard the hymns, the way Phyllis's piano glided along whenever he sang. He remembered corn on the cob, strawberry pie, and the way he had written his initials in wet concrete on the road he had helped Pop Lutz pave. He recalled his first journey to America, his mother's tears at his departure, her joy at his return. He looked at the fractured sky and Phyllis Warner's crinkled face and realized how this ordinary corner of small-town America had shaped his life.

Volkmar Schultz, the German boy, felt his feet become part of the ground, as if his legs had taken root in the old cemetery.

❦

In mid-December we drive Chris to the airport for his return flight to Cape Town. We arrive two hours early, and the boys choose an airport McDonald's for our last meal together. They're a little edgy, and I sense they're nervous about never seeing each other again. There's some talk about meeting before they start college studies, or about Curtis doing an internship at Chris's high school. I'm sad because I know these events are unlikely to happen, but I play along because the boys need to convince themselves it's not the end of their friendship. They have Facebook, Skype, e-mail, and instant messaging, but even these two high-tech whiz kids understand the difference between real life and virtual life. There's a lot you can share online, but cultural understanding? You need to be in the same room, or at least in the same country, for that.

I think about Volkmar and his fifty-year connection to Englewood, Ohio, and wonder if Chris and Curtis will also bond with their exchange communities and families. Both boys have changed for the better as a result of this adventure. Thanks to Chris and his parents, Curtis has returned home fuller and richer, understanding more than I ever did at his age. I hope we've been able to do the same for Chris.

On our way to the security gate we walk past a giant departure board flashing destinations. Istanbul, Shanghai, Tel Aviv, Miami. Dallas, Dubai, Pittsburgh, Paris. There, in the third column, is Chris's flight to Cape Town.

"I used to think Cape Town sounded so far away," says Curtis, with his arm over Chris's shoulder. "And now it seems so close."

"True, that," says Chris.

I can't help it. I start to cry. In a move that seems incredibly mature for his sixteen years, Chris takes my face in his hands, looks into my eyes, and says, "It's okay, Robin. I'll be back."

The kids hug and exchange teen-coded handshakes, and then Chris slings his bag over his shoulder and heads through the X-ray machine. We watch as he continues down the hallway. Already his stride has changed. He was a kid when he arrived here, but as he walks away he seems self-assured and grown-up. He's a man taking the first steps on a long journey home.

The Princess

There's a buzz in the castle lobby this evening.

Visiting dignitaries from a faraway, exotic land checked into Schlosshotel Lerbach last month, and the staff is still pretty excited about having them here. The entourage, which includes a real-life princess, has taken over a dozen of the best guest rooms. Her Highness hails from a part of the world where women, especially royal women, are seldom seen in public, and her presence has bumped the Schloss intrigue up a notch or two. The princess has her own airplane and a fleet of luxury cars and drivers. I see the cars every weekend when I arrive for my piano job—they are shiny and black and royal looking, and parked in formation in a roped-off section of the inner courtyard. The princess has a private entrance to the hotel, and the staff sets up screens so she can negotiate her way to the elevator without anyone seeing her.

Schlosshotel Lerbach has a Michelin three-star restaurant as well as a top-rated hotel kitchen, but the princess has brought her own cook, dishes, and silverware. Several members of the entourage staff a private royal kitchen, built exclusively for the princess in one of the upstairs hallways. I've heard from the housekeeping department that Her Highness's wardrobe, delivered via a large truck, includes new robes and dresses for each of the hundred days she'll be staying with us.

I never see Her Highness, but I know she's here—the scent of myrrh wafts from her living quarters into the main hall of the castle. I daydream while I play the piano and wonder if she's listening. I've tried to learn some popular songs from her country, but it's almost impossible for my Western ears to adjust to the odd intervals and rhythms. I wonder if she has the same problem with my music.

I'm on a first-name basis with Her Highness's security team—not that anyone needs security in this place. I check out the bodyguards, disguised as customers, and wonder if they're packing heat. I could have used a couple of these guys back in New York City—Manhattan hotel lobbies are breeding grounds for stalkers, perverts, and con artists. Nothing criminal ever happens here at the Schloss, except on the nights when they have murder-mystery dinners. Still, it's nice to have the security team around. One never knows when a flying espresso cup or a plate of fois gras might endanger a guest. Or me.

The hotel is filled with purple and dark-pink orchids, because the princess loves them.

Inspired by the spring evening I start my set with a song I wrote called "Magnolia." A guard sits by the fireplace and drinks tea. I wonder where he's hiding his weapon.

Between last night and this evening, the magnolia trees in the park have bloomed, perhaps in honor of Her Highness. The black swans, Kongo and Greta, are swimming around the little lake, and an early spring bride—resplendent in a sugar-plum-fairy dress—has entered the castle from the terrace and graced the lobby with her presence. The brides of May possess a certain sophistication not found in the high-summer brides. They are calmer—more confident and serene. Maybe the scent of magnolia relaxes them.

I play for the bride, I play for the princess, I play for myself, and I play for my daughter, Julia, who has come with me to the Schloss this evening. She also plays the piano and may well be able to sit in for me in a few years. But tonight she's not particularly interested in music. She's hoping to catch a glimpse of the princess, even though I keep explaining that no one ever gets to actually see her.

"How can you be a princess if nobody sees you?" she asks. "Isn't that the whole point?"

"Maybe so," I say. "Who knows—maybe you'll get lucky and she'll appear."

"Wow," she says. "It smells great in here."

"That's myrrh. It's the princess's incense. She's here, even if you can't see her."

"Yep," she says, taking a deep breath of the perfumed air. "There's a princess here. I can feel it."

When I was Julia's age I often fantasized about living in a real European castle. I believed that somewhere beyond the limits of my happy childhood there was a palace with my name on it. My full-service castle included drawbridges and moats, swans and walls of crumbling stone, bathtubs overflowing with bubbles and rose petals, a long staircase for royal entrances into the main hall, and a ghost to humor me and scare away the bad guys. A child of the sixties, I called myself Princess Jackie, after Jackie Kennedy, my idea of an American princess.

Now I've landed here, not exactly in a Camelot kingdom of knights and Kennedys, but in a castle that almost looks like the one from my girlhood dreams. I wonder why I'm here. Have I found the castle or has it found me? I'm sitting behind the piano at the base of the very staircase I once imagined, playing songs for little girls and their grandmothers, young men and their brides, for a genuine princess and her royal family, for my own daughter. I feel as if a small part of my childhood—the dreamy part, the part I thought was gone forever—has returned.

The Schloss park is a *Kinderparadies* with lots of giant trees to climb. Julia's brother, Curtis, once got stuck in a whomping big willow on the castle grounds, and, right in the middle of my sensitive arrangement of "Moon River," I had to leave the piano and climb the tree to rescue him. He ruined his new down jacket, which had gotten stuck on a sharp branch high in the tree, preventing his descent. I ruined a fancy black dress that snagged on the same branch when I unhooked him. This is one reason I hardly ever bring the kids to work with me.

As I play, Herr Jaschke, the general manager, greets Julia and tells her he's about to add a new duck to the family of rare birds swimming on the castle lake.

"Would you like to take pictures?" Herr Jaschke asks. "It should be interesting to see how Kongo and Greta react."

"Of course," says Julia. "I would love to!" She brought her camera hoping to get a picture of Her Highness, but she's too proud to mention that. Besides, in lieu of a princess picture, a duck photo might be just as good.

The Indian Runner Duck—a rare breed known for running instead of waddling—has been sitting in a box in the purchasing office. Within an hour the emotional moment—the release into the wild—will take place. Her Highness has been given the privilege of naming her. After many high-level discussions between hotel management and the princess's staff, a decision has been reached. Her Highness has chosen Sally, a fine name for a duck.

Julia goes outside to prepare for the grand release by hiding in the bulrushes on one side of the water. I keep playing, because the bride is posing for pictures with her family in the lobby and it seems appropriate to provide them a soundtrack. I play "Night and Day." The very young wedding party does not recognize the song—they wouldn't know the difference between Cole Porter and Nat King Cole—but the groom smiles and places a glass of champagne on the piano.

When the photo session concludes, I head outside and stand on the terrace, waiting for the duck release. Herr Jaschke and a member of the royal security team carry the box to the water's edge. They wave toward the terrace, but they're not waving at me. Her Highness must be standing above me at the French doors to her suite. The duck-release team opens the box. Sally jumps into the water and glides across the lake. Indian Runner Ducks are lovely—white with gray and tan markings. Sally isn't running, though, she's swimming, and seems to be content.

But then, before the eyes of the rosy-cheeked bride, numerous castle guests, and my innocent daughter, one of the male ducks—a large Mallard named Dagobert—jumps on Sally and starts to have his way with her. Duck rape. Horrible. Run, Sally, run! Sally does not run. I look at the security guard, half expecting him to shoot Dagobert, or at least dive into the water and tackle him, security-guard style, but he does nothing except watch the show along with everyone else.

An uncomfortable silence, penetrated by occasional squawks, falls over the castle grounds.

After Dagobert finishes his waterfowl foul play with Sally, he swims away, puffed up and cocky. For several moments I think

Sally is, well, a dead duck, but she recovers and begins paddling—cautiously—around the perimeter of the lake. I wonder what Her Highness is thinking. I wonder what Sally is thinking. I know what Julia is thinking because I see her extract herself from her hiding place and stomp back up toward the castle.

I return to the piano and play "Come Fly with Me."

"Well," says Julia as she plops into one of the leather sofas next to the fireplace. "*That* was stupid."

"Did you take pictures?" I ask.

"Are you crazy? I'm not, like, one of those *National Geographic* photographers. I could hardly watch. Poor Sally. What a stupid night. I came to see the princess and instead I have to watch *that?* Geez."

I drift into my second set, playing a medley I call "Songs I Know in the Key of A Major." The wedding guests have moved into the salon for their nuptial dinner. I hope they're not having the *Canard* menu. The night mellows. Lovely people wearing various shades of black and gray pass through the main hall.

I watch my daughter take in the scene, her eyes darting to the staircase, still hoping Her Highness might show up and save the evening.

I'm in the piano zone when all of a sudden Julia jumps up and yells "Nosebleed!" She bunches her scarf over her face and sprints out of the hall.

Never ever take your kids to work.

I keep playing. Julia has frequent nosebleeds, particularly in the spring. She knows what to do and has reached the age where she prefers to attend to the problem without my help. These are not drip-drip episodes, but projectile nosebleeds. They alarm everyone except Julia. I finish the song, discreetly wipe a few drops of blood from the floor, and head down to the ladies' room.

Two elegant women, a blond and a redhead wearing head-to-toe Prada, have Julia stretched out on a long marble counter. They're applying cold compresses to her nose. Julia is trying to be polite, but I can tell she's amused by the attention.

"Excuse me," I say. "I can take over now. Thank you so much for your help."

"This isn't normal," says the blond, completely ignoring me and checking Julia's pulse.

"I think we should call an ambulance," says the redhead.

"I'm okay," says Julia. "It's just a nosebleed! But thank you for your help."

"Where's your mother?" asks the blond.

"I'm her mother," I say.

"Aren't you the pianist?"

"Yes, but I'm also her mother."

"It's true," says Julia. "She's my mother."

"Very nice music."

Another stream of blood gushes out of Julia's nose. The ladies step back to avoid soiling their designer dresses.

"Thank you," I say.

"May I get up?" asks Julia.

"This isn't normal," says the blond

"We should call an ambulance," says the redhead.

"I'm okay," says Julia.

"I'm her mother," I say again. We're on a loop. "These nosebleeds happen *all* the time."

I assure them she's fine, thank them several times, and, finally, they return to their lemon-grass-infused dinners. I will send CDs and a formal thank-you note to their table before we leave. I watch Julia clean her face, and the two of us scrub down the counter and wash basin.

On our way out we walk past the piano. "Mom," she says. "Do you think princesses have nosebleeds?"

"I'm sure they do," I say.

"Oh," she says. "Nosebleeds and princess dresses are not a good match."

"You know, people once believed that royal blood was blue."

"Well," says Julia. "That rules me out."

"I don't know, I think you can still be a princess if you have red blood."

"Do you think Sally is okay?" she asks.

"Let's go see." We step outside.

Sally cruises the lake as if she owns it. Perhaps she's the Buttercup Blondeau of ducks. Or maybe she's a duck princess. Dagobert is on the lawn having a snack. Kongo, Greta, and the other fancy birds, longtime residents of the Schloss park, swim in choreographed circles around Sally, giving her space but staying close enough to make her feel at home. It's the welcome dance of water birds, and we watch as they swim together in the dusky light.

The View from Here

It's a Saturday night in June. I pull into the Schlosshotel Lerbach parking lot, ready to play my regular weekend piano job. Because of the World Cup football frenzy, I expect to find a half-empty castle. But since it's the height of wedding season and there's no stopping a determined summer bride, the hotel is buzzing with well-heeled guests all trying to have a good time, even if many of them would rather be home watching tonight's match.

I'm not much of a sports fan, but—never one to miss an opportunity to look at grown men in Brazilian Boy Scout uniforms—I've been digging the various team outfits. The players look adorable in their multicolored tricots and matching knee socks, and the German coaches, in their lavender silk knit sweaters and perfectly tailored navy blazers, look as if they might be getting ready to play a jazz duo gig at a chichi supper club owned by Calvin Klein. Who's their stylist? Sign me up.

I'll be playing in the main hall tonight. With five minutes to go until my start time, I throw my purse into the back room, change my shoes, adjust the height of the piano bench, grab a glass of water, and head out to the rose garden to see what's going on.

The bride has hired a solo saxophonist to play for her two-hour predinner cocktail party on the terrace. As much as I like the saxophone, I'm not sure that 120 minutes of solo sax is such a great idea. But I admire the bride's resolve to present something a little different. I know the saxophonist, a spunky jazz musician named Thorsten, who's blowing like crazy even though it's boiling hot outside. Thorsten spots me in the doorway and salutes while continuing to play the sax with one hand. Cool guy. It's a wedding gig, so no one is listening to him. Well, really, only about fifty percent of the guests are not listening to him. The other fifty percent have sneaked into the bar to watch the soccer game. Ghana is playing Uruguay tonight. This is a match that makes me wish all countries would adopt the American custom of marching bands at halftime. Imagine a Ghanaian marching band or a drill team from Uruguay. Swinging.

In the banquet room a DJ is setting up to play after-dinner dance music—probably a mix of Gloria Gaynor, Village People, and Donna Summer. I'll be long gone by then, but my coworkers, the hardest-working bunch of young adults in Nordrhein-Westfalen, will be pouring and serving champagne until daybreak.

Time to start playing. I sit down at the grand piano in the lobby and begin my set with Mancini's "Love Theme from Romeo and Juliet." I try to block out the saxophone sound leaking from the garden. Not bad. I'll be fine if I play loudly and don't take too many dramatic pauses.

Boom!

Oh no. The DJ in the dining room is conducting a last-minute sound check, and Celine Dion's voice blasts through the lobby and bounces off the walls. The DJ cranks it up. My God. Does he think this is a football stadium in Cape Town?

I believe your speakers are working, I want to shout. I wait for Celine to stop braying, but she keeps singing about how her heart is going on and on and on. I ask our intrepid banquet manager,

Herr Ries, to put an end to the sound check before Ms. Dion can modulate to an even higher key and my brain explodes. I don't know what Herr Ries does to the DJ—maybe he conks him on the head with an ice bucket—but the music stops abruptly. I continue with "Romeo and Juliet."

The wedding guests float in and out of the lobby. I check out the blushing bride, the little boys in their starched white shirts, and the fresh-as-spring young ladies in their sorbet-colored evening gowns. One dress, a golden-vanilla strapless creation, makes me wonder if I should revamp my Piano Girl wardrobe, but to wear this dress I would need to lose fifteen pounds, have breast reduction surgery and a tummy tuck, and give up playing the piano. Better to stick with the German football coach wardrobe. It's more my style these days.

I play Bach's Air on a G-String. Bad title, but, really, it's a lovely piece of music.

The service staff, smiling and carrying enormous trays of crystal glasses, glides through the lobby, bypassing clumps of guests and dodging the children who dash back and forth in a chocolate-induced race to the front door, where they will be given more chocolate before they streak back to the other side.

I play some music from *The Wonderful World of Amelie*. A sturdy woman in a lace mother-of-the-bride dress smiles at me. I wonder if she actually is the mother of the bride, or just a look-alike.

On top of the piano is a silver urn holding a cluster of eleven dark pink orchids. I know it's eleven, because I count them. God, I love this place—beautiful colors, beautiful clothes, beautiful people. The large window over the staircase diffuses the light and directs it to the lobby, where it hangs in a soft golden stupor. The guests around me dash through the beams, unaware that, for a few moments this evening, they've been airbrushed by the setting sun.

Two men, on their way into the bar to check on Ghana's progress, stop a waitress and ask if they can exchange their champagne for beer.

Four preteen boys discover the antique kicker table in the corner of the lobby. It's a low-tech toy with little hand-operated soccer men. Four players can play at once, two on each side. It's hardly an attraction for a five-star hotel, but this table, made of burled wood and featuring hand-painted players, is more of a hip World Cup art statement than a recreational device.

Klak, klak, klak, klak, klak.

The boys have gathered around the table, and the sound of the little wooden men kicking the ball echoes through the lobby, along with the shouts and cheers of the kids. They're cute for about three and a half minutes, at which point the noise reaches an almost unbearable level. Where are their parents?

Klak, klak, klak, klak, klak.

I'm playing "Moon River."

"TOR!!!!" one of the boys shouts.

I can hear Thorsten playing a blues in a key that clashes with my song.

Klak, klak, klak, klak, klak.

The DJ cranks up Celine again. Her heart is still going on.

"TOR!!!!" the boys yell again.

Monsieur Thomann, the maître d' of the gourmet restaurant on one side of the lobby, peeks through the French doors. He smiles at the boys. Monsieur, the poster child for graciousness, always keeps his temper in check when he's around the guests. He's particularly kind to children.

"*Bonsoir!*" he says to the boys.

"TOR!!!" they scream.

"*Mon Dieu,*" says Monsieur.

Klak, klak, klak, klak, klak.

I give up. I do not blame the boys. They are eleven. In two years they'll be sullen and subdued and doing everything they can to look like gangsters. Let them have their fun. I go to the bar, sip a glass of very nice champagne, watch Ghana score a goal, and thank my lucky stars that I have a job. It's usually so peaceful in this place. One night of extreme noise never hurt anyone, least of all a musician.

⁓

Fifteen minutes later I slip behind the grand piano to begin my second set. The lobby is blissfully quiet. I can see from the piano bench that most of our guests have been seated in their respective dining rooms. Thorsten has finished playing his two-hour saxophone extravaganza, Ghana has won the match and the television has been turned off, the DJ is eating an expensive dinner until it's time for the Titans of Industry disco contest to begin, and the kicker boys have gone to the lake to feed the swans. Monsieur assures me that the kicker ball has mysteriously disappeared for the remainder of the evening.

I play through a selection of original music, songs I like to break out when there's no one listening except me. They are pretty songs from my younger years, with girly-girl names like "Twilight" and "Peaceful Harbor." I close my eyes and play and play and play. I pretend like I'm somewhere else. It's what I know how to do.

Zoom, zoom.

I look up and see a vehicle the size of the Popemobile rumbling through the lobby. Maybe it is the Popemobile; this castle is known for celebrity sightings. Oh no. It's an extremely large electric wheelchair driven by a very assertive-looking middle-aged man. Like most good hotels in Germany, Lerbach accommodates disabled guests, but this is no regular wheelchair—it's huge. The man, who is quite tall, is standing in the vehicle, making it less of a chair and more of a slanted bed with wheels, straps, and a motor. His feet are about at my eye level; the rest of him towers over everything else in the lobby.

I'm playing a piece of mine called "Lerbach Nocturne." I try not to stare at Wheelchair Guy, but I guess if he's riding around in a Popemobile he's used to people gawking at him. A couple of stares from a curious pianist surely won't send him off the deep end. I'm usually good at being discreet, so I avert my eyes and continue playing. But I can't stop looking. I'm stunned by the size of this contraption. Several concerned adults chase after him, but they have trouble keeping up.

Yikes! He almost took out one of the banquet waiters on that last turn.

Zoom, zoom.

I decide that when he passes the piano I will greet him cheerfully, the same way I greet all of our other guests, even though most of our other guests are not riding through the lobby in wheelchairs the size of Hummers. Some of them own Hummers, but they usually keep them in the parking lot next to the smaller cars.

Did he just run over that woman's foot?

Zoom.

Monsieur, who will be seating Wheelchair Guy and his family in the restaurant, stops in his tracks when he sees the size of the vehicle. He smiles, welcomes the guests, then spins on his heels to begin rearranging the restaurant furniture. It's a challenge: a party of four that needs space for sixteen, arriving right in the middle of a sold-out Saturday night.

"Did they call in advance?" I ask one of my coworkers as she passes by the piano.

"Yes," she says. "But they said they were bringing a wheelchair, not a tractor with a hydraulic lift system. The poor guy has to eat standing up. He can't bend. At all."

"Oh no," I say. Words fail me. Now the size of the vehicle makes sense.

I'm still playing "Lerbach Nocturne."

"We would like to have drinks on the terrace," says a member of Wheelchair Guy's party. "So we can enjoy the view."

"I would suggest you have cocktails here in the lobby," says one of the managers. "There's indeed a beautiful view of the park from the bar terrace, but there are steps onto the terrace, so you won't be able to get outside from this direction."

Unless you have a crane, I think. It makes me sad. What a thing— a view that remains invisible because of a few steps. Just as Monsieur turns to talk to the other members of the party, Wheelchair Guy, with what I perceive as a look of defiance—he's so high up I can't see him all that well—steps on the gas and speeds into the bar.

"Good evening," I say as he flies past the piano.

Behind me, I hear a tray of glasses crash to the floor. Then I hear another voice—maybe the bartender's—patiently explain that this part of terrace is not wheelchair accessible. There's no room for a three-point turn in the bar, so Wheelchair Guy, pissed off, backs up at about eighty miles an hour.

Zoom.

It's as if he's being shot out of a cannon backwards. The Popemobile whips into the lobby and crashes into the grand piano so hard that it lurches sideways and pins me to the wall.

"*Mon Dieu!*" says Monsieur.

"Help," I say. The piano is jammed against my upper thigh (thank goodness for fat). My upper arms and elbows are flush against the wall, and my wrists and hands are flapping like little birds in the air over the keys.

I reach down with the tips of my fingers and play the final chords, because, well, I have to end the song. The piano is wobbling and Wheelchair Guy doesn't realize that his Popemobile fender is hooked onto the underside of the piano lid. He jams his shift stick to forward, then reverse, then forward, then reverse. The piano rocks back and forth, and I am certain it is going to crash to the ground, taking me, Wheelchair Guy, Monsieur, and six waiters with it.

"Straight ahead, drive straight ahead, *s'il vous plait,*" says Monsieur to Wheelchair Guy in a firm but pleasant voice. "Straight ahead! Straight ahead!"

"Robin, don't move," says one of the managers. Like I have a choice.

Zoom. Reverse. Zoom. Reverse.

Fuck, fuck, fuck, fuck, fuck.

"Straight ahead!" says Monsieur. "*S'il vous plait!*"

Wheelchair Guy looks down at me. I look up at him. Neither one of us much likes what we see.

Finally, like a desperate mother lifting a Volkswagen off the legs of a trapped child, Monsieur lifts the piano enough to unhinge the Popemobile. It races forward and nearly collides with the tea cart. For a moment I think I've escaped having my legs crushed by a grand piano only to be hit with the world's largest samovar, which is, of course, full of boiling water. But Wheelchair Guy misses the tea cart. Instead, he zigzags to the entrance of the restaurant, followed by the newly appointed Popemobile Task Force, a group of employees designated to prevent more castle damage. A lot can go wrong in a gourmet restaurant, especially when a disgruntled disabled man with a Hells Angels mentality starts zooming around during the soup course.

I am still pinned to the wall. A member of Wheelchair Guy's entourage, a lovely young woman in a perfect black dress, returns to the piano.

"Has the piano been harmed?" she asks, avoiding my eyes.

"I don't know," I squeak. "I'll have to *unpin* myself before I can check out the damage." I wonder why she doesn't ask me if I'm injured. But she hangs out with Wheelchair Guy. Maybe a pianist with a bruised thigh isn't such a big deal.

I heave the piano forward enough to slide out from behind, and limp around to the other side. Amazingly, only a small chunk of wood is missing. The legs are stable. I've always claimed this Yamaha Conservatory Grand is a warhorse; now I know it's true. I wonder if the Popemobile has a dent, a ding, or at least a couple of good battle scars.

A bridesmaid approaches the piano. "Can you tell me where the ladies' room is?" she asks.

"Downstairs," I say.

"Oh! Are you the piano lady? Can you play the theme from *Titanic* for me?"

"Actually, I've finished playing for this evening," I say. I rub my leg. It hurts.

"But you can't stop! I just got here."

"Okay," I say. "I'll be glad to play *Titanic* for you." I sit back down at the piano, start the piece, and she leaves to go to the ladies' room.

That's enough music for me tonight. I head for the bar exit, step onto the terrace, and take in the lush June evening. The trees droop in the weighty heat, but the roses seem plump and content. I walk down a stone staircase to the little lake, where a determined black swan paddles to the other side. Determined. We're all so determined—to have fun, to win the game, to make music, to look good, to get where we want to go.

In the distance I can hear the *thump*, *thump*, *thump* of the DJ's stadium-sized bass speakers. I wonder if the wedding guests are already gearing up for the Electric Slide or the YMCA dance. I wonder if they're celebrating in Ghana. I wonder if Wheelchair Guy is enjoying his gourmet meal, and if the other guests in the dining room are succeeding in their efforts to not stare at him. I wonder if those little boys are now at the front desk, begging the manager to give them another ball. I wonder if Wheelchair Guy ever kicked a soccer ball or played a piano or ate a dinner while sitting in a normal chair. I wonder if he ever danced, or paddled across a pond, or held a glass of champagne.

I skip a stone over the dark green pond and watch each ripple dissolve into the next. When the surface becomes calm again, I look down and see my watery reflection.

Then, because I can, I walk away.

Everyone Here Speaks English

Today I am meeting with the *Oberburgermeister*, the Lord Mayor of Cologne and my only English student. Earlier this year Mayor Roters decided he wanted to improve his English. He gives speeches in English when he's visiting other countries, and he hosts English-speaking dignitaries when they're visiting Cologne. He's a popular and wise politician, with good basic English skills and a broad vocabulary. But he wants more confidence with English small talk at receptions and cocktail parties.

He came to me in a roundabout way. Mr. Mayor's secretary called Amerika Haus—a transatlantic organization dedicated to German-American cultural exchange—and asked the director there, Eveline Metzen, to recommend a conversation partner for her boss. Eveline, who knows I've made my living as a lounge pianist, immediately thought of me.

"Cocktail party chitchat?" said Eveline. "I'll call Robin!"

"Eveline," I told her, "I'm not a teacher. I can play the piano for hours in a hotel bar while people drink cocktails. I can write stories about cocktails and the people who drink them. I can talk about cocktails while I play the piano. I can drink cocktails. I can even make cocktails. But I'm not a teacher for cocktail-party English."

"But he doesn't want a real teacher," she said. "He just wants to talk. You're good at that. Your whole life is a cocktail party."

I don't know if this is a compliment. "Are you sure I'm right for the gig?"

"I'm sure. He's a great guy. Take the job. You'll have fun."

"What do I wear to the *Rathaus*?"

"Just wear what you'd wear to work, you know—a cocktail dress."

I think she's kidding, but I'm not sure. Our first meeting is scheduled for eleven in the morning, and the Audrey Hepburn little black dress is not at all appropriate. So I put on a business suit and my one good scarf, and tuck a notebook under my arm. I look a little boring, but official and somewhat teacher-like.

∽

Many years ago, when we were considering moving to Germany, John sent me a photo of the *Rathaus*.

"Rat house?" I said. "What kind of name is that for City Hall?"

Today I climb the *Rathaus* steps to the *Oberburgermeister's* office. The security guard greets me in English and announces me to the secretary. She takes me in to meet the mayor and stays long enough to serve coffee and cookies.

I'm nervous, Mr. Mayor is nervous, but we're both determined to talk. About something. Anything. As long as it's in English. Cocktail Party 101.

Mr. Mayor hesitates at first, then jumps right in. In the first few minutes he tells me what he hopes to accomplish with our lessons. He doesn't need vocabulary or grammar instruction. He wants to talk—about education, about politics, about food and travel and children. Through unstructured conversations he hopes to eliminate what I call foreign-language brain freeze—that panicky feeling that comes when conversing in a second, third, or fourth language.

I'm hardly an expert, but as far as I can tell, the mayor has the necessary qualifications to meet the language challenge head on. He's willing to make mistakes, he has a sense of humor, and, as a marathon runner, he knows that if he keeps going—in spite of occasionally tripping over the *th*, the *v*, and the *w*—he'll eventually reach the finish line. Still, I know from my own experience learning a foreign language, it will be a very long race.

෴

When we arrived in Germany we spoke only a few words of German, taught to us by a chain-smoking Manhattanite named Brünhilde. She had instructed us to say *"Hier kommt Otto! Otto Schmidt!"* and insisted we learn to count to 100. For weeks I wandered city streets, pushing Curtis in his baby buggy, counting my steps in German, counting the days until we could, at last, meet Otto Schmidt.

"Don't worry about the language," our friends and relatives told us. "Everyone there speaks English." I needed to believe them.

"Moving to a foreign country is like falling in love," said my therapist. "It's a chance to reinvent yourself, a chance to see the world with new eyes, a chance to feel like a kid again."

She didn't mention the *ö.* Nor did she say anything about spending the first five years feeling like an idiot.

At the post office in our old New York City neighborhood, I used to wait in line behind foreigners—Mexican mothers, old men from Serbia, beautiful Korean women—and listen, impatiently, as they struggled to buy a stamp. *Why don't they learn English?* I would think. *It would make their lives so much easier.*

Well. I arrived in Germany and turned into the foreigner at the post office, my ears growing warm with shame, sensing the annoyance of the people behind me as I attempted to buy airmail stickers by stretching my arms out to the side and making airplane noises.

"Oh," said the postal clerk. "You mean *Luftpost.*"

"*Danke,*" I said, grateful to the clerk for not laughing. Maybe this was like falling in love, but I didn't think so at the time.

Every morning at eight thirty John took the bus that took him to the train that took him to work at the WDR recording studio in Cologne. We hadn't yet bought a car, and public transportation in Germany seemed efficient and economical as long as you spoke a little German and knew where you were going. Buses heading in different directions left from one intersection in our neighborhood, and John, wanting to be sure he was on the correct line, always asked the driver if he was going to Rösrath.

"*Fahren Sie nach Rösrath?*" It was a simple-enough phrase, but the bus driver never understood him. The German *r* and *ö* are difficult sounds for Americans. The *r* and the *ö* together were nearly impossible for us.

"Are you headed to *Roosrot?*" he asked.

"Where?" said the driver.

"*Rorssrat,*" said John,

"*Where?*" said the driver.

"*Rossrate,*" said John. No matter how much he practiced before getting on the bus, most days he was forced to pull a map out of his backpack and show the driver the name of the town. It was humiliating.

"Ah," said the bus driver. "You mean *Rösrath.*" Of course the driver got the throaty *r* and the nebulous *ö* just right. The other passengers smirked and stared straight ahead, the quiet arrogance of the native speaker on full display.

The loss of dignity didn't end with the bus ride. Each day at lunchtime John went to the cafeteria to buy a bowl of soup. In order to eat the soup, he had to request a spoon, which cost an extra five cents. But the German word for spoon is *Löffel*, and the cashier, a peevish soupmonger with a wariness of foreigners, refused to give him a *Löffel* unless he said the word correctly.

"Vat do yoo vant?"

"*Ein Loofel, bitte.*"

"*Was?*"

"*Lorffel.* For the soup."

"You have zee soup."

"I know I have the soup. I need the *Lowffel.*"

"*Was?*" she muttered. "I don't understand."

"*LÖFFEL!!!*"

After a month of this, John discovered if he immediately shouted *LÖFFEL* and scared her, she would give him the damn spoon on the first try. But he was the new kid in the cafeteria, and it was degrading to stand there and scream for utensils. In his situation I would have taken my own spoon. Or ordered a sandwich. But John has always liked a challenge.

Brigitte Schweiger, a warmhearted woman I met at a supermarket while trying to decipher the ingredients on a box of cereal, invited me to join a *Krabbelgruppe*, a playgroup for toddlers and their mothers. Twice a week I wheeled Curtis to a neighborhood church where he played and fought with five little boys. The mothers chattered, the boys yelled, and the avalanche of unfamiliar words nearly smothered me. But I kept attending and listening and, eventually, started to identify phrases and understand simple conversations.

We hired a German teacher named Liselotte Lux. She arrived at our house one evening at the designated time and rang the bell. But when we opened the front door, she was not there. We discovered her on her hands and knees in the side garden, emoting over a very large mushroom.

In perfect English she said, "Are you going to eat this?"

"No!" said my husband, horrified.

"Well," she said, "if you don't mind, I'll just take it with me. It will make a delicious dinner!" And with that Liselotte Lux pulled out a pocketknife, lopped off the mushroom at the stem, and plopped it into her handbag.

"You know," I said. "That could be lethal."

Frau Lux laughed. "Oh, I always forget how paranoid Americans are about wild mushrooms." She gave us our first German lesson—about mushrooms—without ever speaking a word of German. Mainly, she wanted to speak English with us. It was a big problem, but we couldn't bring ourselves to fire her. We kept thinking she would die of mushroom poisoning, but every week she returned. After a few months we realized we hadn't gotten past *"Hier kommt Otto Schmidt!"* and started looking for a new teacher.

We blundered through our daily lives, dealing with bankers, auto mechanics, and bakery cashiers who rattled us with rapid-fire responses to our hesitant questions.

"Please," I learned to say in German. "Please speak slowly." With a sympathetic nod, they did.

John hired a teacher named Frau Ernst. The word *ernst* means serious in German, and the name suited her. Frau Ernst showed up twice a week for the next eighteen months. She didn't rummage through our garden looking for fungi, nor did she speak English with us. Instead, with gracious efficiency, she explained German sentence structure, taught us about accusative and dative cases, and encouraged us to converse with her. Never once did she mention Otto Schmidt. John and I gained a working knowledge of German just as I was ready to give birth to our second child.

∽

English has always been my protection, my armor, my waterproof layer of textured wool that keeps me comfortable and dry. German, in spite of all my years of practice, still feels more like an ill-fitting coat from a secondhand store, purchased for me by someone who wasn't sure of my size.

I read somewhere that learning the last twenty percent of a language takes just as long as the first eighty percent. The final part, which includes the ability to speak spontaneously when emotional, seems to take forever. Even though I'll always have my American accent, I'm fine in calm situations. I can hang out with friends for four or five hours and never speak a word of English. I can have a conversation with my children's teachers, negotiate a tricky purchase at a shoe store, book a vacation, or make small talk while I'm playing the piano at a fancy cocktail party. I can even understand our insurance guy when he comes calling, and keep up with our friendly lawyer's legalese. But the minute I get angry or frustrated, my German words, bouncing back and forth from left brain to right, collide with one another and render me unable to form a proper sentence. It's the ultimate disadvantage: I sound stupid when I'm upset.

Today I'm in my car driving in circles, looking for my teenage son, who hasn't shown up at the pickup point outside his school. We are very late for his orthodontist appointment, and, after the third pass around the parking lot, over the bridge, and onto the highway, I'm pretty annoyed. It's only four thirty, but it's getting dark. In Germany it's illegal to make a phone call while driving, so I pull into the bus stop, leave the motor running, grab my phone, and call Curtis. I get his voicemail, so I begin to type a text message.

Rap, rap, rap.

Startled, I look up and see a senior citizen with a cane. He's wearing a pressed jogging suit with neon rainbow stripes on the sleeves, which seems to be the uniform of choice for retired men around here. He raps his cane again on the passenger-side window. Not such a nice thing to do, but I guess he needs directions or help, so I lower the window.

"MOTOR ABSTELLEN!!!!" he screams at me. Turn off your motor. *"UMWELTVERSCHMUTZUNG!!!"* You're polluting the environment.

I glare at him and quickly raise the window. On principle I do not turn off the motor. I take a deep breath. No need to get upset. The sun sinks early on winter days and old men do silly things. I will not lose my temper. I won't.

Rap, rap, rap.

I ignore him and continue writing my text message, although I'm so steamed I've forgotten what I want to write. So I type xxxxxxxxx and hit SEND.

Rap, rap, rap. Now he's banging my windshield with his cane. I pretend to type another message. xxxxxxxx—SEND.

"MOTOR ABSTELLEN!!!! MOTOR ABSTELLEN!!!! MOTOR ABSTELLEN!!!! UMWELTVERSCHMUTZUNG!!!" He keeps rapping.

I turn on the windshield wipers and keep texting. What I really want to do is step out of the car and tell him—in elegant but firm

German—that I'm a stressed-out mom, I'm truly sorry to have left the motor running, but I've spent the last thirty minutes searching for my son, I'm not only angry but a little concerned about his safety, and that *You, sir—even though you are a senior citizen and wearing a freshly laundered Adidas ensemble—you have no fucking right to whack my car with your fucking cane.* But, because I'm angry, my German skills will elude me. I know from experience if I attempt to say any of this in German, he'll make fun of my *Ausländerin* status, laugh at me, and possibly provoke me into doing something with that cane that could get me arrested, deported, or worse.

At first I smile politely. Then I take a deep breath and screech like a warrior, "ARRRRRRRGGGGGGGGGGGGHHHHHHHHH!!!" It's a foreigner's primal scream, and it scares the creases right out of his jogging pants. His face almost blue with rage, he jumps back from my car and scampers away.

I experience a fleeting moment of triumph as I watch him in my rearview mirror. He glances nervously over his shoulder, as if he's afraid I might leap out of the car and clobber him with my datebook. I wait until he's out of sight and turn off my motor. My son comes around the corner, cell phone in hand, and gets in the car.

"What's with the xxxxxx?" he says.

I may have won this round, but I feel like a loser. Oh, how I miss my own language. Right now, as my brain bursts with the many things I should've would've could've said to the man with the cane, I think there would be nothing better than moving back to New York City, Pittsburgh, or even Nantucket. I'm homesick for a place where the right words are there for the taking, where familiar phrases hang in front of my mind's eye like perfect pieces of ripened fruit, ready to be plucked and polished, savored, shared, and understood by those who deserve to hear them.

❧

I've been conversing with Mayor Roters for several months now, and we never run out of things to say. He leads a more privileged life than John and I do. Most of his English-language activities occur in conference rooms, lecture halls, and, yes, at cocktail parties. It's doubtful he'll be pleading with a bus driver, begging a persnickety soupmonger for a spoon, or resorting to primal screaming any time soon. Will he know how to respond in English if a cane-toting man in a jogging suit raps on his car window? Probably not. We'll need a few more lessons before we get that far.

Like me, Mr. Mayor is working on learning that last twenty percent. When he's in town we meet once a week, sometimes twice. He experiences tiny victories, like when he tells a funny story just right, or when he's able to explain a complicated government situation from beginning to end without a single prompt from me. There's a childlike joy to his success. In spite of the huge wooden conference table, the imposing windows overlooking the rooftops of the neighboring buildings, and the three majestic Andy Warhol lithographs of the Kölner Dom hanging on the wall behind him, Mr. Mayor, when he's speaking English, seems like a big kid exploring an even bigger world. The German boy in him takes over and leads the way. The American girl in me understands the challenge. Let's get it right so we can sound like adults.

Let's make the coat fit.

Acknowledgements

I offer my sincere thanks to editor Richard Johnston in Oregon for guiding this book through its final stages. My career has been charmed by many serendipitous events, but finding Richard (or did he find me?) might be the most magical of all.

Nina Lesowitz in California, I adore you. And you look much better in your Clinton photo than I look in mine.

To the Pittsburgh contingent, including Bob and Ann Rawsthorne, Randy Cinski, Curtis Rawsthorne, Jean, Pinky, Marlyn Koehnke, and Debra Todd, I send my love and thanks for your enthusiasm and support. Next time I'm in town I'll meet you all under Kaufman's clock.

To Leslie Brockett Wohlfarth, thank you for always being here for me, even when you're there.

To the New Yorkers—Harlan Ellis, Carol and Emilio Delgado, Pamela Johnson, Peter and Claudia Trivelas, Norman and Ellen Roth, Felice Cohen, Betsy Hirsch, Emilee Floor, Susan Roth, and Greg Thymius—thank you for the inspiration, the welcome-home hugs, the bagels, the laughs, the guacamole, the pull-out sofas and spare bedrooms, the music, the stories, and the chocolate vodka.

A very special thank you to William Zinsser and Marian McPartland, both of whom write and play the piano—an unbeatable combination.

To the gang in Florida, namely Bob Ashley (the most stately member of the Piano Girl fan club) and Frank Baxter, founder and owner of the Piano World Forum, I thank you for cheering me on.

Robin Spielberg in rural Pennsylvania, many thanks for your piano wisdom, friendship, and love. Someday we'll have our two-piano show. Four hands, sounding like two. It will be perfect, as long as we keep our skirts out of the pedals.

Heartfelt thanks to my pals here in Germany, especially Jutta Schmitz, Andrea Goetze, Benedikt Jaschke, Eveline Metzen, Karolina Strassmayer, Tracie Mayer, Katja Bröcher, Heike Bänsch, and Julie Holter.

To Sharon Reamer and Amy Antin, who helped me with early drafts of these stories—I owe you coffee at Buck's for the next 200 years. By the way, have I mentioned how thin you both are looking?

Danke to my German publisher, Alexander Bücken of the Bücken & Sulzer Verlag, for the leap of faith, and to Dagmar Breitenbach for her expert translations. Many thanks as well to Astrid Wahl, Dagmar's sister, for being one of my early readers.

To the team at Schlosshotel Lerbach—you are the best. I'm the luckiest musician in the world to be able to work with you.

All my love to John, Curtis, and Julia Goldsby. Family is family, and you, thank goodness, are mine.

To Conny and Lisa, the little big souls, I think of you every single day. Thank you, wherever you are.

About the Author

Robin Meloy Goldsby is the author of *Piano Girl* and *Rhythm*. Her thirty-year career as a musician has taken her from roadside dives to posh New York City venues and exclusive resorts, and on to the European castles and concert stages where she now performs. Robin has three solo piano recordings to her name—*Twilight, Somewhere in Time*, and *Songs from the Castle*—and has appeared on National Public Radio's *All Things Considered* and *Piano Jazz with Marian McPartland*. Robin is a Steinway Artist. She is also the author and composer of *Hobo and the Forest Fairies*, a musical for children recorded by WDR (Westdeutscher Rundfunk) in Germany. As a lyricist Goldsby has penned songs for Till Brönner, Curtis Stigers, Jessica Gall, Robert Matt, and Peter Fessler. In 2010 her collaboration with singer/composer Joyce Moreno, *Slow Music*, received a Latin Grammy nomination for Best Brazilian Album.

Robin currently lives outside of Cologne, Germany, with her husband—jazz bassist John Goldsby—and their two teenage children.

You can visit Robin Meloy Goldsby's web page at www.goldsby.de. To hear Robin's interviews on *All Things Considered* and *Piano Jazz with Marian McPartland*, please go to www.npr.org/artists.

Made in the USA
Middletown, DE
15 November 2016